HOW
TO GET
WHAT YOU
WANT
FROM THE
U.S.
GOVERNMENT

PATHFINDER PUBLICATIONS, Inc.
Boston, Massachusetts

International Standard Book Number: 0-913390-03-8
Library of Congress Catalog Card Number: 73-82652
Copyright © 1973 by Pathfinder Publications, Inc.
All rights reserved.

Published by Pathfinder Publications, Inc.
108 Massachusetts Avenue
Boston, Mass. 02115

Printed in the United States of America

CONTENTS

INTRODUCTION

In an age when the United States taxpayer asks himself with increasing frequency what the government is doing with his tax dollars, it may be somewhat consoling to realize that many of the programs funded by these tax dollars offer something in return for the money "invested." Despite recent cut-backs in funds, there nevertheless continues to be an abundance of federally-funded programs which directly aid qualified persons.

If the private citizen is reluctant to apply for benefits from such programs, fearing that by doing so he will be stigmatized as a state dependent, he has only to consider the degree to which the government already indirectly assists him in his everyday life—it provides aids to education, it helps to fund highway construction, it maintains its own park system, its own libraries, and its own museums, it provides aids to public health services; the government's influence is seemingly boundless. But often, when an individual considers applying for direct federal aid, he cowers at the thought of being dependent on the government for support.

Conversely, if the private citizen believes that his application for federal assistance might endanger someone else's chances for governmental aid, someone who might be more in need of assistance, he ought to keep in mind that if a government project does not use the funds allocated to it during the course of a fiscal year, it is quite likely that the program's budget will be slashed for the following year. The individual program directors therefore encourage those who are eligible to participate, and the private citizen should therefore feel no compunction about applying to federal programs for aid.

This book is designed to acquaint the reader with many of the programs on which he might capitalize, but because the range of government benefits is so broad, an exhaustive guide to all such aids would be a bulky, unweildy volume marketable only at a price prohibitive to the majority of interested readers. The editors have therefore chosen instead to compile a handy, easy-to-use home reference work outlining a multitude of the more important government programs from which the public may benefit. Each section of the book contains a brief sketch of a particular program, lists eligibility requirements, provides addresses to which inquiries may be made, and suggests other related programs which the reader might care to investigate.

The contents of the book have been chosen so as to appeal to a wide variety of readers—sections deal with educational aids to youth as well as with social security benefits to the elderly, with farm subsidies as well as with small business loans, with rural housing assistance as well as with urban property insurance, with the promotion of the arts and humanities as well as of the sciences, with environmental information as well as with information concerning patents, trademarks, and copyrights, with an outline of consumer protection laws as well as with a summary of civil rights. Finally, Chapter 11 is devoted to some of the agencies within the federal government that offer informational services while the Appendix lists the names and addresses of local and regional offices of government agencies which the reader may wish to consult.

The effectiveness of governmental programs depends on the degree to which the public is informed about these programs and the degree to which the public participates in them. The editors feel that this book will be a convenient starting point from which the reader can be directed to specific information regarding programs of interest to him.

CHAPTER 1

Education

If you're a student or the parent of a student, we don't have to waste your time telling you how expensive higher education is. You already know.

What we will tell you about in this chapter is the large and diverse number of Federal programs that may be able to help you ease the financial pinch of education. These programs include scholarships, loans, fellowships and part-time jobs.

Not surprisingly, the competition is quite stiff for many of these awards. But if you think you have the credentials, don't hesitate to apply. It usually doesn't cost you anything, and, if you're selected, the time will have been well spent.

In addition to examining these Federal educational benefits, students and parents should also thoroughly research the many forms of assistance available from states, towns and private organizations. There are many scholarships and loan funds that qualified students often overlook in their search for financial assistance.

NATIONAL DEFENSE STUDENT LOANS

PROGRAM: In fiscal 1972, it has been estimated that approximately 650,000 graduate and undergraduate students received National Defense (NDEA) loans to assist them in financing their educations. The average to a student was $670. These loans are available at higher education institutions (public, other non-profit, and proprietary) meeting eligibility requirements, such as accreditation.

ELIGIBILITY: Students who need the assistance, can maintain good standing, are enrolled or accepted for enrollment, and are at least half-time students.

HOW TO APPLY: Students should apply directly to the financial aid office at the institution they are attending or wish to attend.

FOR MORE INFORMATION: Program Development Branch
Division of Student Assistance
Bureau of Higher Education
400 Maryland Avenue SW
Washington, D.C. 20202

RELATED PROGRAMS: Educational Opportunity Grants
Guaranteed Student Loan Program
Higher Education Work-Study
Veterans Educational Assistance
War Orphans and Widows Educational Assistance

GUARANTEED STUDENT LOAN PROGRAM

PROGRAM: This mammoth program provides guarantees on loans made for educational expenses by private lenders such as banks, credit unions, savings and loan associations, pension funds and insurance companies (in fiscal 1972, over 1,200,000 loans were guaranteed under this program).

The undergraduate or graduate borrower may have payment deferred while attending an eligible institution on a full-time basis, or, for up to three years, while serving in the U.S. Armed Forces, the Peace Corps, or VISTA.

ELIGIBILITY: Varies from state to state, but, in general, any U.S. citizen, national, or person in the United States for other than a temporary purpose, who is enrolled or accepted for enrollment on at least a half-time basis at an eligible post-secondary school may apply.

HOW TO APPLY: Applications for loans are obtained from and submitted to lenders. The educational institution must certify that the student is accepted for enrollment or enrolled and in good standing.

FOR MORE INFORMATION: Division of Insured Loans
Bureau of Higher Education
Office of Education
Washington, D.C. 20202

RELATED PROGRAMS: National Defense Student Loans

CUBAN STUDENT LOAN PROGRAM

PROGRAM: Cuban nationals who need funds to continue their studies at institutions in this country may be able to obtain long-term low interest loans from the Office of Education. The loans are restricted to $1,000 per academic year and a maximum of $5,000 for undergraduates. For graduates and professionals, the amount is $2,500 a year to a maximum of $10,000.

ELIGIBILITY: Cuban nationals must be attending an educational institution that has established a special Cuban Student Loan Fund. Any institution that participates in the National Defense Student Loan Program is eligible to set up such a fund.

HOW TO APPLY: A student should apply directly to his or her institution by submitting each year Form OE 1061, "Cuban Student's Application for Loan."

FOR MORE INFORMATION: Cuban Loan Section
Program Support Branch
Division of Student Assistance
Bureau of Higher Education
Office of Education
Washington, D.C. 20202

RELATED PROGRAMS: Higher Education Work-Study
National Defense Student Loans

4

LAW ENFORCEMENT EDUCATION PROGRAM (LEEP)

PROGRAM: LEEP provides funds to institutions offering law enforcement courses. These institutions, in turn, make direct loans and grants to students. Loans may not exceed $1,800 per academic year. Grants are for $200 per quarter or $300 per semester and may not exceed the actual cost of tuition, fees, and books.

ELIGIBILITY: Loans are limited to full-time students who enroll in a course of study which will include at least 15 semester credit hours, or the equivalent, in directly related law enforcement courses during the total period of their studies. Loans are forgiven at the rate of 25 per cent for each full year of employment in a public law enforcement agency following completion of school.

Grants are limited to in-service employees of a public law enforcement agency, and certification must be obtained from the employer. Grantees must agree to remain with their currently employing agency for two years following completion of courses.

HOW TO APPLY: Designated student application and note forms may be obtained from institutions receiving LEEP funds.

FOR MORE INFORMATION: Manpower Development
Assistance Division
Office of Criminal Justice Assistance
Law Enforcement Assistance Administration
Department of Justice
Washington, D.C. 20530

RELATED PROGRAMS: Guaranteed Student Loans
Law Enforcement Research
National Defense Student Loans

HIGHER EDUCATION WORK-STUDY

PROGRAM: Higher Education Work-Study (known more simply as the College Work-Study Program) promotes the part-time employment of students, particularly from low-income families, by paying 80 per cent of the money earned by them in qualifying jobs. The students, who must need assistance to pursue courses of study at institutes of higher education, may work up to an average of 15 hours per week during periods of regular enrollment and no more than 40 hours per week at any other time. The work may be either for the institution itself or for any public or private non-profit organization under an arrangement with the institution.

ELIGIBILITY: Full-time undergraduate, graduate or professional students whose resources, including parental contributions, are determined (by the institution in which they are enrolled in good standing or which has accepted them for enrollment as full-time students) to be inadequate to enable them to study at the institution. Non-students, students not in good standing, part-time students, or students not enrolled in eligible institutions are not eligible for the work-study program.

HOW TO APPLY: Students should contact the financial aid office of the educational institution they are attending or wish to attend.

FOR MORE INFORMATION: Program Development Branch
Division of Student Assistance
Bureau of Higher Education
Office of Education
400 Maryland Avenue SW
Washington, D.C. 20202

RELATED PROGRAMS: Educational Opportunity Grants
Guaranteed Student Loan Program
National Defense Student Loans
Vocational Education Work-Study

VOCATIONAL EDUCATION WORK-STUDY

PROGRAM: This program assists economically disadvantaged full-time vocational education students, age 15-20, to remain in school by providing part-time employment with public employers.

ELIGIBILITY: (see Program)

HOW TO APPLY: Students should contact the financial aid office at the school of vocational education that they are attending or wish to attend.

FOR MORE INFORMATION: Division of Vocational and Technical Education
Bureau of Adult, Vocational and
   Technical Education
Office of Education
Washington, D.C. 20202

RELATED PROGRAMS: Higher Education Work-Study

EDUCATIONAL OPPORTUNITY GRANTS

PROGRAM: Educational Opportunity Grants enable students of exceptional financial need to pursue higher education. The grants are for up to four years of undergraduate study and range from $200 to $1,000 per academic year. Furthermore, recipients of these grants must receive at least an equal amount of financial assistance from the institutions they are attending.

ELIGIBILITY: Educational Opportunity Grants may only be awarded by public or private non-profit institutions of higher learning. Colleges or universities must offer at least two years of baccalaureate study; technical or business schools, at least a one-year course of study.

A student receiving an Educational Opportunity Grant must be a national or permanent resident of the U.S., be accepted or enrolled and in good standing for full-time study, and must have an exceptional financing need.

HOW TO APPLY: Students should contact the Director of Financial Aid at the institutions they are attending or wish to attend.

FOR MORE INFORMATION: Program Development Branch
Division of Student Assistance
Bureau of Higher Education
Office of Education
Washington, D.C. 20202

RELATED PROGRAMS: Guaranteed Student Loan Program
Higher Education Work-Study
National Defense Student Loans
Veterans Educational Assistance
Vocational Education Work-Study
War Orphans and Widows Educational Assistance

HIGHER EDUCATION PERSONNEL FELLOWSHIPS

PROGRAM: As a means of increasing the supply of well-prepared teachers, administrators, and educational specialists in areas of critical need for junior-community colleges and four-year colleges and universities, this program provides one- and two-year fellowships for graduate level study. A holder of a fellowship receives $3,000 for each fellowship year plus $500 for each eligible dependent. The institution sponsoring the fellow also receives $3,000 to pay for tuition and non-refundable fees.

ELIGIBILITY: An applicant for a fellowship must be a citizen or national of the U.S. or have status to indicate that he or she is in the country on other than a temporary basis. The applicant must intend to pursue a career in higher education in the United States, its territories and possessions, or Puerto Rico, but must not be in a program which is eligible for support under the National Defense Education Act (NDEA) Fellowship Program.

HOW TO APPLY: Applicants should apply directly to the institution in which they are enrolled or in which they are intending to enroll.

FOR MORE INFORMATION: Bureau of Higher Education
Division of University Programs
Graduate Academic Programs Branch
Office of Education
Department of Health, Education
and Welfare
Washington, D.C. 20202

RELATED PROGRAMS: College Teacher Graduate
Fellowships (NDEA Fellowships)
Promotion of the Arts
Promotion of the Humanities

COLLEGE TEACHER GRADUATE
FELLOWSHIPS (NDEA FELLOWSHIPS)

PROGRAM: The National Defense Education Act (NDEA) provides for the awarding of three-year fellowships to graduate students who intend to become college teachers after completing their doctorate. In fiscal 1972, fellows under this program received average support of $2,500 plus $500 per dependent. Furthermore, fellows do not have to pay tuition or required fees, since institutions must take these expenses out of a cost-of-education allowance awarded to them.

ELIGIBILITY: Graduate students must be American citizens or nationals, or aliens in the process of becoming citizens. Institutions must have an approved doctorate program.

HOW TO APPLY: Institutions nominate students for fellowship support on Office of Education Form 1048, "Application and Nomination for a Graduate Fellowship," in four copies. Student nominees submit one copy of OE Form 4149, "Personal Declaration," to the Headquarters Office listed below.

FOR MORE INFORMATION: Graduate Academic Programs Branch
Division of University Programs
Bureau of Higher Education
Office of Education
Washington, D.C. 20202

RELATED PROGRAMS: Higher Education Personnel Fellowships

NATIONAL DEFENSE FOREIGN LANGUAGE FELLOWSHIPS

PROGRAM: These fellowships are for advanced studies in foreign languages deemed vital to the needs of American education, government and business. The fellowships include tuition, basic stipend, and dependents' allowances, but not travel allowances. No awards are available for study of French, German, or Iberian Spanish, and awards will not be made for summer study only. Academic assistance is at the flat rate of $4,100 for an academic year and $900 for the summer.

ELIGIBILITY: Applicants must hold an undergraduate degree and have been accepted for advanced training in a foreign language and related studies by a graduate school program with a quota of NDFL fellowships. They must be U.S. citizens or resident aliens, must subscribe to the loyalty provisions of the National Defense Education Act, and must be preparing for employment at an institution of higher education in the United States as specialists in certain critical foreign languages or area studies, or for other service of a public nature.

HOW TO APPLY: The student should contact his or her sponsoring institution for information concerning application forms, deadlines and related matters.

FOR MORE INFORMATION: Division of Foreign Studies
Institute of International Studies
Office of Education
ROB-3
7th and D Streets SW
Washington, D.C. 20202

RELATED PROGRAMS: Teacher Exchange

PROMOTION OF THE ARTS

PROGRAMS: The National Foundation On The Arts and The Humanities provides grants to support innovative programs in the arts. These grants are generally of the "matching" variety, meaning that the individual or organization must provide an equal amount of money for the project.

ELIGIBILITY: Individuals and non-profit organizations are eligible to apply for these grants.

HOW TO APPLY: Contact the National Endowment for the Arts for specific application procedures. Specify the particular area of interest.

FOR MORE INFORMATION: National Endowment for the Arts
806 15th Street NW
Washington, D.C. 20506

RELATED PROGRAMS: Promotion of the Humanities

PROMOTION OF THE HUMANITIES

PROGRAMS: The National Endowment for the Humanities provides financial support, in the form of fellowships, stipends, and research grants, to assist outstanding humanists realize their potential as scholars and teachers. Categories of fellowship programs include younger humanists, junior college teachers, minority studies, fellowships for the professions, and senior fellowships. Younger humanists may also apply for summer stipends.

ELIGIBILITY: In general, U.S. citizens are eligible to apply.

HOW TO APPLY: For specific eligibility guidelines and application procedures, contact the National Endowment for the Humanities, specifying the particular area of interest.

FOR MORE INFORMATION: National Endowment for the Humanities
Washington, D.C. 20506

RELATED PROGRAMS: Promotion of the Arts

LIBRARY FELLOWSHIPS

PROGRAM: This program enables institutions of higher education to offer graduate fellowships in librarianship and also to conduct institutes in that field.

ELIGIBILITY: Persons who have been engaged in or are presently engaged in librarianship, or persons who have a degree in library science, or persons concerned with the study or teaching of library or information science, or persons who are preparing to engage in a profession or other occupation involving librarianship, including library paraprofessionals.

HOW TO APPLY: Institutions apply for the fellowships, so individuals should apply directly to the institutions.

FOR MORE INFORMATION: Division of Library Programs
Bureau of Libraries and
   Educational Technology
Office of Education
400 Maryland Avenue SW
Washington, D.C. 20202

RELATED PROGRAMS: Higher Education Personnel Fellowships

FELLOWSHIPS IN HEALTH RESEARCH

PROGRAMS: The National Institutes of Health award research fellowships in many categories (allergies and infectious diseases, arthritis, cancer, child health, dental research, environmental health services, eye research, general medical sciences, heart and lung research, neurological diseases and strokes, and nursing research). Fellowships are generally designated as postdoctoral or special, with a few predoctoral fellowships also awarded. Fellowships cover a basic stipend and tuition costs, with a dependency allowance included in the postdoctoral category.

ELIGIBILITY: Postdoctoral candidates must possess an M.D., D.D.S., Ph.D., D.V.M., Sc.D., D.Eng. or equivalent advanced degree in the applied science area. (Fellowships will not be awarded for study which leads to a professional degree.)

Applicants for special fellowships generally must possess a doctorate and have three subsequent years of research or professional experience.

HOW TO APPLY: Applications should be obtained from and returned to the Career Development Review Branch at the address below.

FOR MORE INFORMATION: Career Development Review Branch
Division of Research Grants
National Institutes of Health
Bethesda, Maryland 20014

RELATED PROGRAMS: Health Professions Assistance
Health Services Research Fellowships
Nursing Assistance

MENTAL HEALTH FELLOWSHIPS

PROGRAM: These fellowships are intended to provide support for training for research relating to the problems of mental illness and mental health. The predoctoral, postdoctoral and special fellowships provide a stipend based on the individual's training and experience, dependency allowances where applicable, and other necessary expenses. An allowance is also made to the sponsoring institution to cover tuition, fees, and other costs of research training. The average fellowship award is $7,000.

ELIGIBILITY: An applicant for a fellowship must be a citizen or national of the United States or must have been lawfully admitted for permanent residence. The individual must qualify by scholastic degree and previous training or experience for the level of support sought. Each applicant must be supported by an institution with an adequate program and facilities for research training.

HOW TO APPLY: Required application forms and instructions may be obtained from the Behavioral Sciences Training Branch, Division of Manpower and Training Programs, National Institute of Mental Health.

FOR MORE INFORMATION: Behavioral Sciences Training Branch
Division of Manpower and Training Programs
National Institute of Mental Health
5600 Fishers Lane
Rockville, Maryland 20852

RELATED PROGRAMS: Mental Health Information

OCCUPATIONAL HEALTH FELLOWSHIPS

PROGRAM: The Health Services and Mental Health Administration awards these special fellowships to individuals committed to careers in research and teaching and the application of research findings relevant to occupational safety and health.

ELIGIBILITY: Applicants for a special fellowship must have either (1) at least three years of relevant research or professional experience after receiving the doctorate, or (2) otherwise demonstrated sufficient competence to pursue the proposed training program. The applicant must also have a demonstrated commitment to occupational safety and health by virtue of previous training, experience and/or recognized contribution in the field.

HOW TO APPLY: PHS Form 416-1 should be completed and returned to the National Institute for Occupational Safety and Health (office listed below).

FOR MORE INFORMATION: Office of Extramural Activities
National Institute for Occupational
   Safety and Health
Department of Health, Education, and Welfare
550 Main Street
Cincinnati, Ohio 45202

RELATED PROGRAMS: Fellowships in Health Research

HEALTH PROFESSIONS ASSISTANCE

PROGRAMS: Students pursuing training in the health fields of medicine, dentistry, osteopathy, optometry, podiatry, pharmacy, or veterinary medicine may apply for financial assistance in the form of scholarships and long-term low interest loans. $3,500, whether in the form of a scholarship or a loan, is the maximum amount of assistance in any one academic year.

ELIGIBILITY: Students must be enrolled in a full-time program at an accredited institution leading to a degree in one of the health professions.

HOW TO APPLY: Students should apply to the financial aid office at their school.

FOR MORE INFORMATION: Grants Management Staff
Division of Physician and Health
  Professions Education
Bureau of Health Manpower Education
National Institutes of Health
9000 Rockville Pike
Bethesda, Maryland 20014

RELATED PROGRAMS: Nursing Assistance

NURSING ASSISTANCE

PROGRAMS: Nursing students who require aid to enter and complete a program of nursing education may apply under these programs for scholarships and/or long-term low interest loans. The maximum amount of a scholarship is $2,000 a year, while the maximum amount of a loan is $2,500 annually and $10,000 total. Up to 85 per cent of loans to nursing students may be cancelled under specific conditions of employment as a registered nurse.

ELIGIBILITY: Applicants must be full- or half-time nursing students in good standing or have been admitted for at least half-time study in a nursing education program. Students must be United States citizens or have been admitted to the country for permanent residence.

HOW TO APPLY: Nursing students should contact the financial aid office of the institution at which they are studying or to which they have been admitted.

FOR MORE INFORMATION: Division of Nursing
Bureau of Health Manpower Education
National Institutes of Health
9000 Rockville Pike
Bethesda, Maryland 20014

RELATED PROGRAMS: None

HEALTH SERVICES RESEARCH FELLOWSHIPS

PROGRAM: Fellowships for individuals doing health services research provide for stipend support, dependency allowances, tuitions, and supply allowances.

ELIGIBILITY: U.S. citizens or nationals, or foreign nationals lawfully admitted to the country for permanent residence.

HOW TO APPLY: A candidate must be sponsored by an institution (e.g., university, hospital, etc.) with an adequate program and facilities for this kind of research. Applications must be made on Form PHS 416-1, Research Fellowship Application.

FOR MORE INFORMATION: National Center for Health Services Research
and Development
Health Services and
Mental Health Administration
Department of Health, Education and Welfare
5600 Fishers Lane
Rockville, Maryland 20852

RELATED PROGRAMS: Fellowships in Health Research

WATER POLLUTION FELLOWSHIPS

PROGRAM: The Environmental Protection Agency awards research fellowships for advanced study in the field of water pollution control, including disciplines such as environmental engineering, water chemistry, and pollution-oriented biology, physical and social sciences. Funds are available for stipends and allowances based on level or type of fellowship.

ELIGIBILITY: Qualified individuals with Master's degrees are eligible for fellowships.

HOW TO APPLY: Requests for application forms and completed applications should be submitted to the headquarters office listed below.

FOR MORE INFORMATION: Grants Administration Division
Environmental Protection Agency
Washington, D.C. 20460

RELATED PROGRAMS: Air Pollution Fellowships

AIR POLLUTION FELLOWSHIPS

PROGRAM: These fellowships are intended to increase the number and competence of professional personnel engaged in research and other activities related to the prevention and abatement of air pollution. The fellowships, which run between $5,000 and $6,000, cover tuition and fees, stipends, dependancy allowances, and travel.

ELIGIBILITY: Applicants must have a bachelor's degree from a recognized institution or equivalent experience and must have been accepted for admission in an advanced program.

HOW TO APPLY: Requests for application forms and completed applications should be submitted to the Washington, D.C. headquarters office.

FOR MORE INFORMATION: Grants Administration Division
Environmental Protection Agency
Washington, D.C. 20460

RELATED PROGRAMS: Water Pollution Fellowships

FULBRIGHT-HAYS PROGRAM

PROGRAM: This program provides grants to enable American students to live and study in a foreign country for one academic year (with possible renewals or extensions). Full grants cover round-trip transportation, a language or orientation course, tuition, books, maintenance for the academic year, and health and accident insurance.

ELIGIBILITY: Applicants should be American citizens who hold a B.A. degree or its equivalent. They should have language proficiency sufficient to communicate with the people of the host country and to carry out their proposed studies.

HOW TO APPLY: Applicants who are enrolled in American colleges and universities should contact the Fulbright-Hays program adviser on campus.

FOR MORE INFORMATION: Institute of International Education
809 United Nations Plaza
New York, N.Y. 10017

RELATED PROGRAMS: None

SMITHSONIAN EDUCATION AND RESEARCH TRAINING PROGRAMS

PROGRAM: The Smithsonian Institution offers appointments annually in the fields of natural history, science and technology, American culture, history and art. The purpose of these appointments is to serve as recognized academic experience for predoctoral and postdoctoral scholars, as well as undergraduate and graduate students. In addition to fellowships, a limited number of stipends plus certain allowances are available.

The formal structure of the Smithsonian program allows study under the disciplines of History of Science and Technology, American and Cultural History, History of Art and Music, Anthropology, Evolutionary and Systematic Biology, Environmental Sciences, Tropical Biology, and Physical Sciences. The program also includes direct research in Smithsonian collections and libraries, professional staff consultation, direction and instruction, and related seminars and conferences.

ELIGIBILITY: Appointments with fellowship support are available to (1) postdoctoral scholars and scientists within five years of their Ph.D., to pursue further training in research; (2) doctoral candidates to conduct research for their dissertations with approval of their university departments; and (3) graduate and undergraduate students as summer research participants under the direction of Smithsonian professional staff members. Individuals are also eligible for appointment without stipend to the program in museum study for training in museum skills and research techniques.

HOW TO APPLY: Obtain application forms and guidelines from the Office of Academic Studies, Smithsonian Institution (address below).

FOR MORE INFORMATION: Office of Academic Studies
Smithsonian Institution
Washington, D. C 20560

RELATED PROGRAMS: None

NUCLEAR EDUCATION AND TRAINING

PROGRAMS: If you're a student or teacher working in the field of nuclear science, you may be able to receive significant financial assistance and specialized instruction from the Atomic Energy Commission. The AEC provides fellowships in the areas of nuclear science and radiation protection. It also arranges for faculty-student conferences and experiments, research experience for both undergraduate and graduate students, an honors program for senior science majors, and workshops and summer institutes for faculty members.

ELIGIBILITY: In general, science and engineering faculty and students.

HOW TO APPLY: Contact the Atomic Energy Commission for specific application procedures and eligibility requirements.

FOR MORE INFORMATION: Division of Nuclear Education and Training
U.S. Atomic Energy Commission
Washington, D.C. 20545

RELATED PROGRAMS: None

LAW ENFORCEMENT RESEARCH

PROGRAM: Doctoral candidates engaged in dissertation research on a problem related to the criminal justice system (preferably a criminal justice manpower problem) are eligible to apply for fellowship stipends and tuition and fees reimbursement.

ELIGIBILITY: The doctoral candidate must be a citizen of the United States and may not receive any other direct Federal educational benefit, with the possible exception of veteran's benefits.

HOW TO APPLY: The format used to apply will be made available by the Manpower Development Assistance Division.

FOR MORE INFORMATION: Manpower Development Assistance Division
Office of Criminal Justice Assistance
Law Enforcement Assistance Administration
Washington, D. C. 20530

RELATED PROGRAMS: Guaranteed Student Loans
Law Enforcement Education Program
National Defense Student Loans

CITIZENSHIP EDUCATION

PROGRAM: Would you like to become a naturalized citizen? If you attend citizenship education courses under the supervision of a public school or public educational institution, you will have the free use of Federal textbooks on citizenship. These textbooks, which are at various reading levels, are designed for use in acquiring or expanding a knowledge of English, U. S. history, government and basic citizenship responsibility.

ELIGIBILITY: Aliens attending public citizenship classes are eligible to receive free use of Federal textbooks. Persons who cannot qualify for free textbooks may purchase copies from the Government Printing Office.

HOW TO APPLY: Information on citizenship programs may be obtained from any Immigration and Naturalization Service office.

FOR MORE INFORMATION: Immigration and Naturalization Service
Department of Justice
119 D Street NE
Washington, D.C. 20536

RELATED PROGRAMS: None

TEACHER EXCHANGE

PROGRAM: Under this program, qualified American teachers receive opportunities to teach abroad for an academic year in elementary or secondary schools or to attend summer seminars abroad.

Grants to teach abroad provide round-trip transportation for some countries; no transportation is provided for dependents. Maintenance allowance, paid in the currency of the host country, is based on that country's cost of living; in some cases the recipient's U.S. salary is continued. Subject to available funds, supplemental dollar grants ranging from $800 to $2,500 may be awarded to teachers going to certain countries.

Grants for attendance at seminars provide round-trip transportation; participants in some seminars are responsible for their own maintenance expenses. No dependents are to accompany teachers participating in seminars.

ELIGIBILITY: Elementary and secondary school teachers, college instructors, and assistant professors. Applicants must have at least a bachelor's degree and must be U.S. citizens at time of application. Candidates must have at least three years of successful full-time teaching experience to qualify for a teaching position abroad; two years for summer seminars, and must be currently teaching. Evidence of good health and emotional maturity and stability is required.

HOW TO APPLY: Applications should be submitted on forms available on request from the Headquarters Office listed below.

FOR MORE INFORMATION: Teacher Exchange Section
Division of International Exchange and
   Training
Institute of International Studies
Office of Education
ROB-6
7th & D Streets SW
Washington, D. C. 20202

RELATED PROGRAMS: National Defense Foreign Language Fellowships

TEACHER CORPS

PROGRAM: The Teacher Corps provides programs where interns acquire practical experience in schools serving low-income children. As part of their internship, Corpsmen take courses in education (free of cost to them) at nearby colleges and universities, at either the graduate or undergraduate level. Members of the Teacher Corps receive stipend payments during their service (up to two years).

ELIGIBILITY: College graduates and persons with at least two years of college are eligible to apply for the Teacher Corps.

HOW TO APPLY: Individuals seeking to apply for positions in the Teacher Corps should write to the nearest recruitment and referral center as follows: Western Center, 1031 Broadway, Room 1150, Los Angeles, California 90015; Northeastern Center 1343 H Street NW, Suite 902, Washington, D.C. 20005; Southeastern Center, C&S Bank Building, Room 605, Athens, Georgia 30601; Great Lakes Center, 5271 Cass, Detroit, Michigan 48202; and Midwestern Center, 3805 North 16th Street, Omaha, Nebraska 68110.

FOR MORE INFORMATION: Teacher Corps
Bureau of Educational Personnel Development
Office of Education
Washington, D.C. 20202

RELATED PROGRAMS: Teacher Exchange

CHAPTER 2

Social Services

Social Security.
Unemployment Insurance.
Food Stamps.

These are some of the Federal programs that most people take for granted—unless circumstances cause them to have to apply for the benefits. Then they realize that life would be a lot harder without such essential Government social service programs.

Read this chapter carefully, whether or not you intend to apply for any of the benefits at the immediate moment. We bet it will be a pleasant surprise for you to realize the number of programs Uncle Sam has available when you need them.

SOCIAL SECURITY DISABILITY INSURANCE

PROGRAM: The Social Security Administration pays monthly cash benefits to replace part of the income that a person loses when he or she is not able to work because of a physical or mental impairment. Costs of vocational rehabilitation are also paid for certain beneficiaries. No payments are made for the first six months of a disability.

ELIGIBILITY: A disabled worker under age 65 is eligible for Social Security disability benefits if he or she has worked for a sufficient period of time under Social Security. (The requirements depend upon the age of the applicant and the date of disability.) A disabled widow 50 or over is eligible if her deceased husband was covered by Social Security. (This also applies to disabled widowers and certain disabled surviving divorced wives.)

The following categories of *dependents* of disabled workers are also eligible for cash benefits: (1) unmarried children under 18; (2) children 18 through 21 if unmarried and full-time students; (3) unmarried disabled children 18 or over if disabled before 18; (4) wife at any age if a child in her care is receiving benefits on the worker's Social Security record; and (5) wife or dependent husband 62 or over.

HOW TO APPLY: Telephone or visit the local Social Security office.

FOR MORE INFORMATION: Bureau of Disability Insurance
Room 760
Social Security Administration
Baltimore, Maryland 21235

RELATED PROGRAMS: "Black Lung" Benefits
Life Insurance for Veterans

SOCIAL SECURITY RETIREMENT INSURANCE

PROGRAM: Social Security provides for monthly cash payments to eligible retired workers and their eligible dependents. There are no restrictions on use of the payments by beneficiaries.

ELIGIBILITY: If you have worked the required number of years under Social Security, you become eligible for retirement benefits at age 62, but you will receive larger payments if you do not apply before age 65.

Classes of dependents eligible for payments include (1) a wife or dependent husband 62 or over; (2) a wife of any age with dependent children in her care if the child is entitled to payment based on the worker's record; (3) unmarried children under 18 (22 if in school); and (4) unmarried disabled children 18 and over who were disabled before 18.

HOW TO APPLY: Telephone or visit the local Social Security office.

FOR MORE INFORMATION: Bureau of Retirement and Survivors Insurance
Room 500
Social Security Administration
Baltimore, Maryland 21235

RELATED PROGRAMS: "Black Lung" Benefits
Social Security Benefits for Persons 72 and Over
Social Security Survivors Insurance

SOCIAL SECURITY BENEFITS FOR PERSONS 72 AND OVER

PROGRAM: The purpose of this program is to assure some regular income to certain persons aged 72 and over who had little or no opportunity to earn Social Security protection during their working years.

ELIGIBILITY: Individuals who reached age 72 before 1968 need no work credits under Social Security to be eligible for special monthly payments. Those who reached that age during or after 1968 need some work credits to be eligible, with the specific amount increasing gradually each year (for person reaching 72 in that year) until it will be the same as that required for ordinary Social Security retirement benefits. Special payments can also be made under this program to an eligible wife aged 72 or over.

No payments are made in any month in which an otherwise eligible person receives a payment under a Federally-ordered public assistance program. These monthly payments are also reduced by the amount of any other governmental pension, retirement benefit or annuity.

HOW TO APPLY: Telephone or visit the local Social Security office.

FOR MORE INFORMATION: Bureau of Retirement and Survivors Insurance
Room 500
Social Security Administration
Baltimore, Maryland 21235

RELATED PROGRAMS: Social Security Retirement Insurance
Social Security Survivors Insurance

SOCIAL SECURITY SURVIVORS INSURANCE

PROGRAM: When a person who has worked under Social Security dies, this program pays monthly cash benefits to eligible dependents.

ELIGIBILITY: Benefits are payable only if the deceased had enough wage credits. Dependents eligible for monthly cash benefits are the following: (1) any widow 60 or older; (2) a widow of any age if she is caring for a child under 18 or disabled, and the child gets payments; (3) unmarried children under 18 (22 if in school); (4) unmarried disabled children 18 or over, if the disability occurred before age 18; (5) a widow or dependent widower 50 or older who becomes disabled not later than seven years after the death of the worker; (6) a dependent widower 62 or older; and (7) dependent parents 62 or older.

HOW TO APPLY: Telephone or visit the local Social Security office.

FOR MORE INFORMATION: Bureau of Retirement and Survivors Insurance
Room 500
Social Security Administration
Baltimore, Maryland 21235

RELATED PROGRAMS: "Black Lung" Benefits
Death Compensation and Pension
Life Insurance for Veterans

MEDICARE

PROGRAM: Medicare provides hospital insurance protection to persons over 65. Under this program, persons may enroll, for a monthly charge, for supplementary medical insurance as well as for the basic coverage, for which there is no cost.

ELIGIBILITY: Persons 65 or over, whether retired or working.

HOW TO APPLY: Telephone or visit the local Social Security office.

FOR MORE INFORMATION: Bureau of Health Insurance
Room 700
Social Security Administration
Baltimore, Maryland 21235

RELATED PROGRAMS: Social Security Disability Insurance

"BLACK LUNG" BENEFITS

PROGRAM: Coal miners who have become totally disabled due to pneumoconiosis (black lung disease) may receive monthly cash benefits to replace the income lost as a result of the disease. Widows of miners who died of black lung disease may also receive benefits, as may children if no widow survives.

ELIGIBILITY: In order to be eligible for payments, a miner must have become "totally disabled" from black lung disease (even though he may still be able to work outside of coal mines).

HOW TO APPLY: Telephone or visit your local Social Security office.

FOR MORE INFORMATION: Bureau of Disability Insurance
Social Security Administration
6401 Security Boulevard
Baltimore, Maryland 21235

RELATED PROGRAMS: Social Security Disability Insurance
Social Security Survivors Insurance

UNEMPLOYMENT INSURANCE

PROGRAM: This program provides financial benefits to unemployed workers. The benefits are paid on a weekly system for a period generally not in excess of 26 weeks over a period of a year, beginning approximately when the first claim is filed. Benefits are extended up to an additional 13 weeks when unemployment reaches specified levels on either a state or national basis.

ELIGIBILITY: All workers whose employers have contributed to state unemployment insurance programs. Federal civilian employees and ex-servicemen are eligible if they are involuntarily unemployed, registered and ready for work, and meet the earnings requirement of the state law.

HOW TO APPLY: Register for work and file a claim for unemployment benefits at a local office of the state employment service.

FOR MORE INFORMATION: Unemployment Insurance Service
Manpower Administration
Department of Labor
Washington, D.C. 20210

RELATED PROGRAMS: Employment Service

NARCOTIC ADDICT TREATMENT

PROGRAM: The Federal Government maintains hospitals in Lexington, Kentucky and Fort Worth, Texas where eligible addicts may be committed for up to six months of hospital treatment. After sufficient improvement, the addict may be placed in a rehabilitation program providing 2 1/2 years of after-care under the supervision of a community social agency.

ELIGIBILITY: Individuals eligible for commitment are (a) narcotics addicts charged with certain Federal offenses who wish to be committed for treatment in lieu of prosecution; (b) addicts convicted of a Federal crime who are sentenced to commitment; and (c) addicts not charged with a crime who apply for commitment to treatment themselves or for whom petition is made by a related individual.

An individual must be committed for examination to determine whether he or she is an addict and is likely to be rehabilitated before acceptance will be given into the program.

HOW TO APPLY: Through Federal court petition.

NOTE: *Since many addicts enter this program mainly to escape a jail sentence, the "cure" rate traditionally has not been high. There are now state, local, and private addict programs in almost every major city and many smaller ones.*

FOR MORE INFORMATION: Division of Narcotic Addiction and Drug Abuse
National Institute of Mental Health
Health Services and Mental Health
    Administration
5600 Fishers Lane
Rockville, Maryland 20852

RELATED PROGRAMS: Alcohol and Drug Dependence Service
Mental Health Information

MENTAL HEALTH INFORMATION

PROGRAMS: If you need information in the Mental Health area, it's a good bet that the Department of Health, Education and Welfare can supply what you want.

The Department runs two clearinghouses: The National Clearinghouse for Mental Health Information and the National Clearinghouse for Drug Abuse Information. Types of public information materials and activities range from brochures, fliers, fact sheets, pamphlets and exhibits, news releases and news features, as well as films, television and radio productions, articles for national magazines, and daily assistance to representatives of the public media. Both clearinghouses have become the foremost computerized repositories of mental health and related research findings in the world.

In addition, the Secretary's Committee on Mental Retardation (SCMR) has been established as the focal point for coordination and information on all aspects of HEW's mental retardation program, as well as for general information about mental retardation.

ELIGIBILITY: Anyone is eligible to receive information.

HOW TO APPLY: Verbal or written request.

FOR MORE INFORMATION: Office of Communications
National Institute of Mental Health
Health Services and Mental Health
   Administration
5600 Fishers Lane
Rockville, Maryland 20852

or

Secretary's Committee on Mental Retardation
Department of Health, Education, and Welfare
Washington, D.C. 20201

RELATED PROGRAMS: Alcohol and Drug Dependence Service
Mental Health Fellowships
Narcotic Addict Treatment

BOOKS FOR THE BLIND AND PHYSICALLY HANDICAPPED

PROGRAM: The Library of Congress provides library service, in the form of talking books, books in braille, and talking book machines, to blind and physically handicapped residents of the United States and its territories. There are 50 regional libraries in this country with a collection of approximately 26,000 titles in recorded and braille form and 23,000 music scores in braille.

ELIGIBILITY: An applicant must provide a certificate of inability to read or manipulate conventional printed material from a competent authority (normally a doctor of medicine, an ophthalmologist, or an optometrist, but may also include registered nurses, professional staffs of hospitals, rehabilitation centers, and health and welfare agencies).

HOW TO APPLY: Applications can be made to the Division for the Blind and Physically Handicapped in Washington or through one of the 50 regional libraries. Information on the regional libraries is available from any public library.

FOR MORE INFORMATION: Division for the Blind and Physically Handicapped
Library of Congress
1291 Taylor Street NW
Washington, D.C. 20542

RELATED PROGRAMS: None

CAPTIONED FILMS FOR THE DEAF

PROGRAM: The Office of Education maintains a free loan service of captioned films and instructional media for the educational, cultural, and vocational enrichment of the deaf.

ELIGIBILITY: State or local public agencies and schools, or organizations of deaf persons are eligible.

HOW TO APPLY: Apply to the Media Services and Captioned Films Branch of the Bureau of Education for the Handicapped at the address below.

FOR MORE INFORMATION: Media Services and Captioned Films Branch
Office of Education
Department of Health, Education and Welfare
Washington, D.C. 20202

RELATED PROGRAMS: Books for the Blind and Physically Handicapped

SPECIAL PROGRAMS FOR CHILDREN WITH LEARNING DISABILITIES

PROGRAM: The Office of Education awards funds for the establishment and operation of model centers for the improvement of education of children with specific learning disabilities, through research and training of educational personnel.

ELIGIBILITY: Public or non-profit agencies, organizations, or institutions may receive grants.

HOW TO APPLY: By letter to the Associate Commissioner, Bureau of Education for the Handicapped, Office of Education, 400 Maryland Avenue SW, Washington, D.C. 20202.

FOR MORE INFORMATION: Program Development Branch
Division of Educational Services
Bureau of Education for the Handicapped
Office of Education
400 Maryland Avenue SW
Washington, D.C. 20202

RELATED PROGRAMS: Books for the Blind and Physically Handicapped
Captioned Films for the Deaf

POSTAL STREET ACADEMIES

PROGRAM: The United States Postal Service operates street academies in six major cities (Atlanta, Chicago, Detroit, Newark, San Francisco, and Washington, D.C.). The purpose of these academies is to recruit and train school dropouts for employment in industry and Government or for entrance into college.

ELIGIBILITY: Applicants must be 16 to 22 years old and be able to benefit from the academies because of a present lack of employment, under-employment, or incomplete education.

HOW TO APPLY: To the Postal Academy Director/Trainer in the cities having Postal Academies.

FOR MORE INFORMATION: Postal Academy Program
Office of Social Priorities
U.S. Postal Service
1100 L Street NW
Suite 4135
Washington, D.C. 20260

RELATED PROGRAMS: Vocational Education Work–Study

EMPLOYMENT SERVICE

PROGRAM: The United States Employment Service and affiliated state employment services operate over 2,300 local offices to serve those seeking or needing employment and those providing it. General services include outreach, interviewing, testing, counseling and referral to placement.

Special services are offered to veterans, the disadvantaged, the handicapped, older workers, and persons living in rural areas.

ELIGIBILITY: Everyone is eligible.

HOW TO APPLY: Contact the nearest local office of the state employment service.

FOR MORE INFORMATION: Employment Service
Manpower Administration
Department of Labor
Washington, D.C. 20210

RELATED PROGRAMS: Civil Service Employment
Federal Employment for Disadvantaged Youth
Federal Employment for the Handicapped
Federal Employment Preference for Veterans

CIVIL SERVICE EMPLOYMENT

PROGRAM: A lot of people work for Uncle Sam. If you'd like to join them, in most cases you will have to pass a competitive examination. The requirements for specific positions vary in relation to the duties performed. All Civil Service positions in Federal agencies must be filled without discrimination because of race, religion, sex, politics, or any other nonmerit factor. Veterans receive preference on examinations.

ELIGIBILITY: Any U.S. citizen may apply. There is no maximum age limit. The usual minimum age limit is 18.

There are special programs (listed separately) to help place the physically handicapped, the mentally retarded or mentally restored, and the disadvantaged. An arrest record does not automatically bar a person from Federal employment.

HOW TO APPLY: Application forms are available from Job Information Centers at area offices of the U.S. Civil Service Commission.

FOR MORE INFORMATION: Federal Job Information Center
U.S. Civil Service Commission
1900 E Street NW
Washington, D.C. 20415

RELATED PROGRAMS: Employment Service
Federal Employment for Disadvantaged Youth
Federal Employment for the Handicapped
Federal Employment Preference for Veterans
Federal Summer Employment

FEDERAL EMPLOYMENT FOR DISADVANTAGED YOUTH

PROGRAMS: The Civil Service Commission sponsors programs which provide employment in Federal agencies for disadvantaged young people, aged 16 through 21. Both full-time employment during the summer and part-time work during the school year are available.

ELIGIBILITY: Students must meet the financial need criteria of the programs. No special skills or experience are required. Students hired for part-time work during the school year must maintain an acceptable school standing.

HOW TO APPLY: Students should contact their guidance counselors or the youth division of the local office of the state employment service.

FOR MORE INFORMATION: Office of Youth Employment Programs
Bureau of Recruiting and Examining
Civil Service Commission
Washington, D.C. 20415

RELATED PROGRAMS: Employment Service
Federal Summer Employment

FEDERAL EMPLOYMENT FOR THE HANDICAPPED

PROGRAM: The Federal Government provides employment opportunities to the physically handicapped, the mentally retarded and the mentally restored in positions for which they can qualify. A Selective Placement Program is specifically directed toward the utilization of all groups of handicapped persons in selected positions. This program deals with referral, placement, trial appointments, and the retention of Federal employees who become disabled for one position, but may qualify for others.

ELIGIBILITY: Persons with physical or mental disabilities who are interested in Federal employment.

HOW TO APPLY: Handicapped persons or rehabilitation personnel working in their behalf should contact the nearest regional or local office of the Civil Service Commission or the coordinator for selective placement at a local Federal agency.

FOR MORE INFORMATION: Public Policy Employment Programs
Manpower Sources Division
Bureau of Recruiting and Examining
Civil Service Commission
Washington, D.C. 20415

RELATED PROGRAMS: Employment Service

FEDERAL SUMMER EMPLOYMENT

PROGRAM: If you're a student, you probably know how hard it is to get a summer job that is meaningful and pays a good salary. Have you considered trying for a summer job in a Federal agency?

Most agencies employ college students, as well as high school students with special skills, during summer vacation periods. The jobs may be clerical, crafts and trades, administrative or subprofessional related to career interests. Summer employees receive the regular Federal pay rate for the positions they fill.

ELIGIBILITY: Any U.S. citizen may apply. The minimum age requirement is 18 years at time of appointment to a summer job. This requirement is waived, however, for high school graduates who are at least 16 years old at time of appointment.

Most summer jobs with Federal agencies are filled through eligibility established through a nationwide examination given during the winter or early spring.

HOW TO APPLY: Application forms and instructions are available at Job Information Centers or Civil Service regional offices.

FOR MORE INFORMATION: Federal Job Information Center
Civil Service Commission
1900 E Street NW
Washington, D.C. 20415

RELATED PROGRAMS: Federal Employment for Disadvantaged Youth

FOOD STAMPS

PROGRAM: Food stamps or "coupons" may be bought by needy families. The coupons, which are worth more than the purchase amount (which varies according to income and family size) may then be used to buy food in retail stores. The stamps may be used to buy any food for human consumption, except items labeled as imported. Almost all grocery stores in food stamp areas are authorized to accept coupons.

ELIGIBILITY: Families may participate if they live in an area that has the program, are found by local welfare officials to be in need of food assistance, are receiving some form of welfare assistance, and are unemployed, part-time employed, working for low wages, or living on limited pensions. If families are not receiving welfare assistance, eligibility is based on family size, income, and level of resources.

HOW TO APPLY: Families in areas where the food stamp program is in operation should apply to their local welfare offices.

FOR MORE INFORMATION: Food Stamp Division
Food and Nutrition Service
Department of Agriculture
Washington, D.C. 20250

RELATED PROGRAMS: Food Donations

FOOD DONATIONS

PROGRAM: You may be eligible to receive surplus food directly from the Federal Government.

ELIGIBILITY: Families must live in a city or county which has a Food Donation program and must be certified by local welfare authorities as having inadequate income and resources. The family head may be employed, pensioned, striking or unemployed. Upper limits of allowable income vary with family size and among local jurisdictions.

HOW TO APPLY: Individuals or heads of households should apply to local welfare authorities or approved health facilities.

FOR MORE INFORMATION: Food Distribution Division
Food and Nutrition Service
Department of Agriculture
Washington, D.C. 20250

RELATED PROGRAMS: Food Stamps
School Food and Milk Programs

SCHOOL FOOD AND MILK PROGRAMS

PROGRAM: The Department of Agriculture reimburses public and non-profit private schools (high school and under) for costs of providing free or reduced price breakfast, lunch and milk to children unable to pay the full cost. The breakfasts and lunches must meet nutritional requirements prescribed by the Secretary of Agriculture. No discrimination, physical or otherwise, may be made against any child receiving food or milk at less than full price.

ELIGIBILITY: Children determined by local school authorities to be unable to pay the full cost of any of these programs.

HOW TO APPLY: Parents should consult with local school officials to see if their children are eligible.

NOTE: *No hungry child can learn well in school.*

FOR MORE INFORMATION: Child Nutrition Division
Food and Nutrition Service
Department of Agriculture
Washington, D.C. 20250

RELATED PROGRAMS: Food Donations
Food Stamps

COMMUNITY RELATIONS SERVICE

PROGRAM: The Community Relations Service (CRS) helps communities and groups cope with disputes, disagreements and difficulties arising from racial discrimination or inequities. The professional staff of CRS seeks to persuade and encourage local citizens and institutions to take the initiative in solving their own problems. In addition to helping to resolve on-going disputes, CRS also seeks to solve problems before they destroy the peace. CRS may enter a community on its own initiative or upon request.

ELIGIBILITY: Any person, group, community, or state or local governmental unit that seeks to alleviate conditions caused by discrimination based on race, color, or national origin may be considered for CRS assistance.

HOW TO APPLY: Applicants for assistance may write, phone, or personally contact national or field offices. No standard form is used.

FOR MORE INFORMATION: Community Relations Service
Department of Justice
Washington, D.C. 20530

RELATED PROGRAMS: See programs listed in section on civil rights.

CHAPTER 3

Housing

You've decided it's time to buy a house. Do you know the different kinds of Federal mortgage insurance programs that can keep your interest rates down?

Or maybe you already own a house, and you want to make those major repairs that you've been putting off. Uncle Sam has some low-cost programs that can save you money. Do you know what they are?

Are you tired of conventional houses? How about living in a mobile home? The Government provides insured loans to make purchase easier. (In fact, most of the Federal loan programs, especially in the housing area, do not consist of direct loans to the borrower, but, rather, insurance for the lender which, in turn, brings down the rate of interest charged to the borrower.)

These are a few of the Federal housing programs that dollar-conscious citizens take advantage of every year. If you'd like to join them, read this chapter carefully. You may be the richer for it.

INTEREST SUBSIDIES

PROGRAMS: In order to make home ownership more readily available to lower-income families, the Department of Housing and Urban Development (HUD) administers programs in which interest subsidies are paid directly to lenders of FHA-insured mortgage loans. These monthly assistance payments to the lenders serve to reduce the effective interest rate paid by lower-income homeowners to as little as 1 per cent.

These subsidized mortgage loans may be used to finance the purchase of a single-family home, a two-family home, or a unit in a multi-family structure which has been (a) constructed or substantially rehabilitated no more than two years prior to the application for assistance or (b) rehabilitated by a nonprofit sponsor after approval from HUD.

Maximum insurable loans for an occupant mortgagor under these programs are: one-family home, $18,000, or up to $21,000 in high cost areas; two-family home, $24,000, or up to $30,000 in high cost areas. For a large family, the limit for a single home is $21,000, or up to $24,000 in high cost areas.

For eligible families, the downpayment may be as low as $200. Assisted families are required to pay at least 20 per cent of their adjusted income (gross income after certain allowable deductions) for mortgage payment. Mortgage terms may extend for 30 years, or 35-40 years if the mortgagor is unacceptable under a 30-year term. Interest reduction payments may extend for the full mortgage term, but stop when the assisted family's income exceeds the maximum allowable for receiving the benefits of the subsidy.

ELIGIBILITY: Families eligible to apply for mortgage insurance and receive the benefits of the subsidies must fall within certain income limits and meet other criteria (as determined by locality on a case by case basis) as explained in program literature.

HOW TO APPLY: Applications, along with any necessary supporting evidence, should be submitted to the local HUD office through the approved mortgage lender.

FOR MORE INFORMATION: Housing Production and Mortgage Credit/FHA
Department of Housing and Urban
   Development
Washington, D. C. 20410

RELATED PROGRAMS: Mortgage Insurance
Public Housing—Home Ownership for
   Low-Income Families

PUBLIC HOUSING—HOME OWNERSHIP FOR LOW-INCOME FAMILIES (TURNKEY)

PROGRAM: Low-income families living in public housing developments have an opportunity under this program to eventually own their own homes.

Here's the way it works: HUD will credit the amount the local public agency budgets for routine maintenance to family equity accounts, provided that in return, such maintenance is performed by the tenants. When a family's income increases to the point where permanent financing for the unit is possible, or when the family's equity account equals the unamortized debt and closing costs, ownership passes to the family. Originally the units are owned (Turnkey III) or lease (Turnkey IV) by the local public agency.

A unit can be part of a planned development, condominium, or cooperative. During the period of tenancy under this program, families must make payments of between 20 and 25 per cent of their income. Turnkey III homes are amortized over a period of up to 30 years, while Turnkey IV assistance is for up to 20 years.

ELIGIBILITY: Local housing authorities established by a local government in accordance with state law, authorized public agencies, and Indian tribal organizations are eligible to administer these programs for low-income families with a potential for home ownership.

HOW TO APPLY: Prospective homeowners should contact the local public agency.

FOR MORE INFORMATION: Publicly Financed Housing Division
Housing Production and Mortgage Credit
Department of Housing and Urban
 Development
Washington, D.C. 20410

RELATED PROGRAMS: Interest Subsidies

LOW TO MODERATE INCOME
HOUSING LOANS
(RURAL HOUSING LOANS)

PROGRAM: The Farmers Home Administration (not to be confused with the Federal Housing Administration) has provided guaranteed or insured loans to assist rural families in obtaining decent, safe and sanitary dwellings.

A dwelling financed for a family with a low or moderate income must be modest in size, design and cost. Interest credits may be granted to lower-income families to reduce the effective interest rate to as low as 1 per cent.

ELIGIBILITY: Citizens or permanent residents of the United States who either own a farm or, when the loan is closed, will become the owner of a farm or nonfarm tract in a rural area. Persons must have adequate and dependably available income to meet operating and family living expenses. They must, however, lack sufficient resources to provide by themselves the necessary housing, buildings and related facilities, and they must be unable to secure the necessary credit from other sources at reasonable terms.

HOW TO APPLY: An indefinite moratorium has been placed on new applications for this and other subsidized housing programs. Any office of the Farmers Home Administration will be able to supply the latest information on the status of the moratorium.

FOR MORE INFORMATION: Farmers Home Administration
Department of Agriculture
Washington, D.C. 20250

RELATED PROGRAMS: Rural Housing Disaster Loans
Rural Rental Housing Loans
Very Low Income Housing Repair Loans

MORTGAGE INSURANCE

PROGRAMS: To keep the interest rates on mortgages low and thereby encourage home ownership, HUD, through its Federal Housing Administration, insures lenders against loss on many of the mortgages they finance. Following are the mortgage insurance programs most commonly utilized by individuals.

HOME: This is the mainstay of the mortgage insurance program, with 222,990 mortgages insured in fiscal 1971 alone. Loans may be used to finance the purchase of proposed, under construction, or existing one-to-four family housing, or to refinance indebtedness on existing housing. Maximum insurable loans for an occupant mortgagor are $33,000 for a one family house, $35,750 for a two or three family house, and $41,250 for a four family house.

In most instances, the maximum amount of the loan will be 97 per cent of the first $15,000 of estimated value, 90 per cent of the next $10,000 and 80 per cent of the amount over $25,000. The downpayment is the difference between the maximum loan amount and the purchase price of the house, with the purchaser also responsible for all items of prepaid expense (such as taxes).

The current maximum insurance rate for all mortgage programs, unless otherwise stated, is 7 per cent plus 1/2 per cent for the mortgage insurance premium. The FHA application fee for these programs is $40 for existing and $50 for proposed housing. The service charge by the mortgagee varies but may not normally exceed 1 per cent of the purchase price. The mortgage terms, unless otherwise stated, may extend for 30 years or three-fourths of the dwelling's remaining economic life, whichever is less, or 35 years if the mortgagor is unacceptable under a 30-year term and, in some cases, if the property has been constructed subject to FHA or VA inspection.

HOMES FOR LOW AND MODERATE INCOME: Loans guaranteed or insured under this plan may be used to finance the purchase of proposed or existing low-cost one-to-four family housing or the rehabilitation of such housing. Maximum insurable loans for an occupant mortgagor are $18,000 for a one family house ($21,000 in high-cost areas). For large families (five or more persons), the limit is $21,000 ($24,000 in high-cost areas). Higher mortgage limits are available for two-to-four family houses.

For most families, the maximum amount of the loan is the appraised value of the house or 97 per cent of the appraised value plus prepaid expenses, whichever is less. The downpayment is the difference between the maximum loan amount and the purchase price of the house plus prepaid expenses. Families who have previously been displaced by urban renewal or other government action are eligible for lower rates, but must make a minimum downpayment of $200.

53

HOMES IN OUTLYING AREAS: Loans may be used to finance the purchase of proposed, under construction, or existing one family nonfarm housing or new farm housing on five or more acres adjacent to a highway. The maximum insurable loan for an occupant mortgagor is $16,200.

HOMES IN URBAN RENEWAL AREAS: Loans may be used to finance the acquisition or rehabilitation of one to 11 family houses in approved urban renewal or code enforcement areas. Properties must be constructed or rehabilitated in accordance with an approved urban renewal plan. The maximum insurable loans for occupant mortgagors are the same as under the basic program of mortgage insurance for homes, as are the downpayment rates and length of mortgage terms. Veterans are eligible to receive special rates in this category.

HOMES IN OLDER, DECLINING AREAS: Loans may be used to finance the purchase, repair, rehabilitation and construction of housing in older, declining urban areas where conditions are such that certain normal eligibility requirements for mortgage insurance under a particular program cannot be met. Property must be an acceptable risk, within the context of the need for providing adequate housing for low and moderate income families.

Mortgages for housing eligible under this special program may be insured under any one of several FHA programs. The maximum amount of the loan, the downpayment, and other mortgage terms vary according to the FHA program under which the mortgage is insured.

SPECIAL CREDIT RISKS: Loans may be used to finance the purchase and/or rehabilitation of new or existing single family homes. Maximum insurable loans for an occupant mortgagor are $18,000, or $21,000 in a high-cost area.

The downpayment and term of the mortgage are determined by the requirements for the particular FHA program under which the application originates.

Buyers whose mortgages are to be insured under this program may also qualify for interest subsidies paid monthly by the FHA to the mortgagee, which may reduce the effective interest rate paid by the homebuyer to as little as 1 per cent.

The application fee for special credit risk mortgage insurance is $45 for proposed and $35 for existing housing.

MORTGAGE INSURANCE FOR VETERANS: (described in Veterans section).

MORTGAGE INSURANCE FOR DISASTER VICTIMS: (described in Disaster Relief section).

PURCHASE OF CONDOMINIUMS: Loans may be used to finance the acquisition of individual units in proposed or existing condominium projects containing four or more units. An individual mortgagor may not own more than four units purchased with FHA-insured mortgages.

The maximum insurable loan for an occupant mortgagor is $33,000. If a family is also eligible for interest subsidies, the maximum loan is 100 per cent of the estimated value, and the downpayment is $200. The FHA application fee is $40, but is waived if the application has been filed before an issuance of a commitment to insure the project mortgage.

FEE SIMPLE: Loans may be used to finance the purchasing by homeowners of fee simple title to properties held under long-term leases on which their homes are located. The maximum insurable loan is the cost of purchasing the fee simple title or $10,000 per family unit, whichever is less. The maximum amount of a specific loan is equal to the difference between the maximum amount prescribed for homes and the current indebtedness on the property, subject to the $10,000 limitation.

The FHA application fee is $20. The mortgage terms may extend for 20 years or three-fourths of the remaining economic life, whichever is less.

ELIGIBILITY: All families are eligible to apply for the mortgage insurance program which they feel best suits their needs. Exceptions are the special credit risks and fee simple programs.

Mortgage insurance for special credit risks is available only to persons who do not qualify for home ownership under regular FHA credit standards. Families qualifying under this program must have a gross monthly income at least four times the amount of the required monthly mortgage payment.

Only homeowners whose residences are located on properties which are held under long-term leases are eligible to apply for fee simple mortgage insurance.

Families displaced by urban renewal or other government action are eligible for special rates in the mortgage insurance program for homes for low and moderate income persons. Certification of eligibility for the special terms is made by the appropriate local government agency.

HOW TO APPLY: Applications should be submitted for review and approval to an HUD Insuring or Area office by an FHA-approved mortgagee.

In the case of mortgage insurance for special credit risks, the prospective homeowner must obtain counseling assistance from an HUD-approved counseling agency before his application may be submitted by the mortgagee. Information regarding the availability of counseling assistance may be obtained from HUD Area and Insuring offices.

FOR MORE INFORMATION: Assistant Commissioner for Unsubsidized
Insured Housing Programs
Housing Production and
Mortgage Credit/FHA

Department of Housing and
Urban Development
Washington, D.C. 20410

RELATED PROGRAMS: Housing for Totally Disabled Veterans
Interest Subsidies
Low to Moderate Income Housing Loans
Major Home Improvement Loan Insurance
Mortgage Insurance for Disaster Victims
Mortgage Insurance for Veterans

MOBILE HOME LOAN INSURANCE

PROGRAM: To provide reasonable financing of mobile home purchases, the Federal Housing Administration insures lenders against losses on loans made for these purposes. A buyer must intend to use the mobile home as his or her principal place of residence. The maximum amount of a loan is $10,000 ($15,000 if two or more modules are to be financed). The downpayment required is low, and finance charges range from 7.63 to 10.57 per cent annually, depending on the amount and term of the loan.

ELIGIBILITY: All persons are eligible to apply. A borrower must give assurance that his or her unit will be placed on a site which complies with FHA standards and with local zoning requirements.

HOW TO APPLY: Application for a mobile home loan should be submitted to an FHA-approved lender for review and approval. The FHA itself does not normally participate in the approval or disapproval of individual loans.

FOR MORE INFORMATION: Assistant Commissioner for Property
Improvement
Housing Production and Mortgage
Credit/FHA
Department of Housing and Urban
Development
Washington, D.C. 20410

RELATED PROGRAMS: Property Improvement Loan Insurance
Veterans Housing Loans

RENT SUPPLEMENTS

PROGRAM: Lower-income families may be eligible to have part of their monthly rental costs subsidized by the Federal Housing Administration. Assistance covers the difference between the tenant's payment and the market rental, but may not exceed 70 per cent of the market rental. Payments are made monthly to the owners of approved multifamily rental housing projects. Assisted tenants must pay at least 25 per cent of their adjusted monthly income (after certain deductions) for rent.

ELIGIBILITY: Families must be within income limits (as determined by locality on a case by case basis) prescribed for admission to public housing in order to qualify for benefits under this program. Others may occupy units in a rent supplement project, but must pay the full rent.

HOW TO APPLY: An indefinite moratorium has been placed on this and other subsidized housing programs. Any Housing and Urban Development Office will be able to supply the latest information on the status of the moratorium.

FOR MORE INFORMATION: Assistant Commissioner for Subsidized Housing
            Programs
            Department of Housing and
            Urban Development
            Washington, D. C. 20410

RELATED PROGRAMS: Interest Subsidies
            Low to Moderate Income Housing Loans
            Mortgage Insurance
            Very Low Income Housing Repair Loans

RURAL RENTAL HOUSING LOANS

PROGRAM: The Farmers Home Administration provides guaranteed or insured loans to help finance rental and cooperative housing for rural residents.

Loans may be used to construct, purchase, improve, or repair rental or cooperative housing. Such housing may consist of apartment buildings, duplex units, or individual houses. Funds may also be used to provide recreational and service facilities appropriate for use in the dwellings and to buy and improve the land on which the buildings are to be located. Loans may not be made for nursing, special care, or institutional-type homes.

ELIGIBILITY: Applicants may be individuals, cooperatives, nonprofit organizations, or corporations unable to finance such housing either with their own resources or with credit obtained from private sources. The applicants, however, must be able to assume the obligations of the loan, furnish adequate security and have sufficient income for repayment. They will be required, in addition, to present a comprehensive market analysis showing the need for such rental housing.

HOW TO APPLY: An indefinite moratorium has been placed on new applications for this and other subsidized housing programs. Any office of the Farmers Home Administration will be able to supply the latest information on the status of the moratorium.

FOR MORE INFORMATION: Farmers Home Administration
Department of Agriculture
Washington, D.C. 20250

RELATED PROGRAMS: Farm Labor Housing Loans
Mortgage Insurance

VERY LOW INCOME HOUSING REPAIR LOANS (SECTION 504 HOUSING LOANS)

PROGRAM: This program supplements the Low to Moderate Income Housing Loans program by providing direct loans for very low income rural homeowners who want to make essential minor repairs on their homes. Loans may be used for repairs on the foundation, roof or basic structure as well as water and waste disposal systems.

The maximum amount of a loan for the improvement of one rural residence is generally $2,500. An additional $1,000 can be authorized if improvement involves the buying or installing of a water or waste disposal system or plumbing supplies for the bathroom or kitchen. Loans may not be made to assist in the construction of new dwellings or farm buildings.

ELIGIBILITY: An applicant must own and occupy a farm or rural nonfarm tract; lack sufficient income to qualify for a Low to Moderate Income Housing Loan (also known, bureaucratically speaking, as a Section 502 Loan); have no reasonable prospect of improving income to a qualifying level for such a loan; but have enough income to repay a Section 504 Loan.

HOW TO APPLY: Application forms are available at local Farmers Home Administration offices.

FOR MORE INFORMATION: Farmers Home Administration
Department of Agriculture
Washington, D.C. 20250

RELATED PROGRAMS: Low to Moderate Income Housing Loans
Major Home Improvement Loan Insurance
Property Improvement Loan Insurance

HOUSING REHABILITATION

PROGRAMS: The Department of Housing and Urban Development awards grants for the rehabilitation of certain residential properties. Loans are also available for this purpose, for both residential and business properties.

These funds may be used to rehabilitate property located in federally assisted code enforcement areas, urban renewal areas, areas certified for later renewal, and for properties deemed uninsurable because of physical hazards in areas under a statewide Fair Access to Insurance Requirements (FAIR) plan.

ELIGIBILITY: Owner-occupants of residential properties (up to 4 units) are eligible to apply for grants. When the grantee's income exceeds $3,000 a year, the grant may be reduced if the housing expense is less than 25 per cent of his income.

Eligible to apply for loans are owners or tenants of property in neighborhood development, urban renewal and code enforcement areas. In certified areas, however, loans may be made only to an owner-occupier of residential property.

HOW TO APPLY: For grants, HUD Form 6260 should be submitted to the local agency sponsoring the program. Submit HUD Forms 6230 or 6234 for loans on residential property and HUD Form 6247 for a loan on nonresidential property.

NOTE: *These programs are scheduled to be replaced in fiscal 1973 by Urban Community Development Revenue Sharing, but will continue to be funded if revenue sharing is not enacted.*

FOR MORE INFORMATION: Community Development
Department of Housing and
 Urban Development
451 7th Street SW
Washington, D.C. 20410

RELATED PROGRAMS: None

MAJOR HOME IMPROVEMENT LOAN INSURANCE

PROGRAM: Families wishing to repair or improve existing residential structures that are located outside of urban renewal areas may apply for low cost loans insured by the Federal Housing Administration.

Loans may be used for alterations of existing one-to-four family housing. The housing must be at least 10 years old unless the loan is primarily for major structural improvements. The maximum insurable loan on a single-family structure is $12,000 or $17,400 in areas where cost levels so require.

The current maximum interest rate is 7 per cent plus 1/2 per cent for the mortgage insurance premium. The FHA application fee is $20. The service charge by the lending institution varies, but may not normally exceed 1 per cent of the total loan.

ELIGIBILITY: Everyone is eligible to apply.

HOW TO APPLY: Apply through an FHA-approved mortgagee, who will forward the papers to a HUD Insuring or Area Office.

FOR MORE INFORMATION: Assistant Commissioner for Unsubsidized Insured Housing Programs
Housing Production and Mortgage Credit/FHA
Department of Housing and Urban Development
Washington, D.C. 20410

RELATED PROGRAMS: Housing Rehabilitation
Mortgage Insurance
Property Improvement Loan Insurance
Very Low Income Housing Repair Loans

PROPERTY IMPROVEMENT LOAN INSURANCE

PROGRAM: If you need some money to fix up your home, an FHA-insured loan might come in very handy. These loans may be used either to finance alterations, repairs or improvements for existing structures or to finance construction of proposed nonresidential, nonfarm buildings.

The maximum amount of a property improvement loan is $5,000, except for multi-family structures where the ceiling is $2,500 per unit, up to a limit of $15,000. Finance charges vary from 8.83 to 10.57 per cent annually, depending on the amount and term of the loan.

ELIGIBILITY: Eligible borrowers are the owner of a property or a lessee having a lease extending at least six months beyond the maturity of the loan.

HOW TO APPLY: Apply directly to an FHA-insured lender.

FOR MORE INFORMATION: Assistant Commissioner for Property Improvement
Housing Production and Mortgage Credit/FHA
Department of Housing and Urban Development
Washington, D.C. 20410

RELATED PROGRAMS: Housing Rehabilitation
Loan Insurance for Construction of Nonresidential Farm Structures
Major Home Improvement Loan Insurance
Mortgage Insurance
Very Low Income Housing Repair Loans

URBAN PROPERTY INSURANCE

PROGRAM: Under prodding by the Federal Insurance Administration (FIA), State Fair Access to Insurance Requirements (FAIR) Plans have been set up in 26 states, the District of Columbia and Puerto Rico. These plans are designed to assure reasonable access to basic property insurance (fire, extended coverage, and vandalism and malicious mischief) to any property owner in an urban area.

(The FIA's leverage has been its policy of providing Federal reinsurance against excessive losses from riots and civil disorders only to property insurance companies that cooperate as risk-bearing members of a FAIR Plan.)

ELIGIBILITY: Owners of property in urban areas with FAIR plans. The property must be found insurable (upon inspection); the premium rate depends upon the physical condition of the property without regard to environmental hazards.

HOW TO APPLY: Property holders unable to get coverage through the normal insurance market should contact the office of the state FAIR plan or the state insurance commissioner.

FOR MORE INFORMATION: Federal Insurance Administration
Department of Housing and Urban
   Development
Washington, D.C. 20410

RELATED PROGRAMS: Crime Insurance
Flood Insurance

FLOOD INSURANCE

PROGRAM: A major flood can literally wash away everything in its path. To provide financial protection to property owners, the Department of Housing and Urban Development offers flood insurance at a premium lower than the actuarial rate would be for the area.

The maximum amounts of coverage are $17,500 for a single-family house and $30,000 for a structure containing two or more family units, plus a $5,000 limit per unit for contents. For all other properties, there is an aggregate liability of $30,000 for any single structure, plus $5,000 for contents per occupant.

In communities in which actuarial rates have previously been determined, a second, equal layer of coverage may be purchased at the actuarial rate. Owners of properties built or substantially improved after identification as an area of special flood hazard may purchase insurance at the actuarial rates only, in amounts not exceeding the maximums available for existing properties.

ELIGIBILITY: Flood insurance under this program may be made available to states or areas which have (1) provided official evidence of their interest in the coverage and (2) have adopted adequate land use and control measures.

HOW TO APPLY: Individuals interested in obtaining flood insurance should consult the appropriate HUD area office or local HUD insuring office, or their State Commissioner of Insurance.

NOTE: *A 40 per cent reduction in the cost of this flood insurance went into effect in June, 1972 following the disastrous floods that ravaged the Maryland and Pennsylvania areas. For instance, a homeowner may now purchase $10,000 of flood insurance for $25 a year, as compared to the previous yearly rate of $40.*

FOR MORE INFORMATION.:   Federal Insurance Administration
Department of Housing and Urban
   Development
Washington, D.C. 20410

RELATED PROGRAMS: Crime Insurance
River and Flood Forecasts
Urban Property Insurance

CHAPTER 4

Business

Do you have a small business that you'd like to see get bigger? Do you know what services the Small Business Administration offers to start you moving in the right direction?

Are you looking for some more customers? Uncle Sam does a lot of business each year with private companies. The General Services Administration can give you some good tips on the procedures that must be followed to obtain Government contracts.

Are you thinking of doing business overseas? The Bureau of International Commerce may be just the place for you to get the preliminary information you need.

What we're saying is that Uncle Sam thinks it's good business to give a hand to private enterprise. Turn the page and start learning what Federal benefits you can take advantage of in your business.

SMALL BUSINESS SERVICES

PROGRAMS: "If my company weren't so small . . ."

The Small Business Administration (SBA) cannot transform your business from a little acorn to a big oak. But it does offer a variety of programs designed to help small companies compete more successfully in the business world. The following are the Small Business Administration services most likely to be utilized by individuals.

SMALL BUSINESS LOANS: This program provides both direct and guaranteed/insured loans (over one billion dollars of the latter in 1972) to construct, expand, or convert facilities; to purchase building equipment, or materials; or for working capital.

Funds must not otherwise be available on reasonable terms. They may not be used to pay off a loan to an unsecured creditor in a position to sustain loss, nor may they be used to effect change in the ownership of the business, or to indiscriminately relocate it.

ECONOMIC OPPORTUNITY LOANS (EOL): Direct or guaranteed/insured loans of up to $25,000, with a maximum maturity of 15 years, may be made to low-income or socially or economically disadvantaged persons to assist them in establishing, preserving, and strengthening small businesses. Funds must not otherwise be available on reasonable terms.

DISPLACED BUSINESS LOANS: These loans are available to most small businesses which have suffered physical displacement and/or economic injury as a result of a Federally-aided urban renewal, highway, or other construction project. Loans may be used to continue in business, purchase a business, or establish a new business.

Funds may not be used for speculation, non-profit enterprises, selling business to strangers, paying off principals or unsecured creditors, holding real property primarily for sale or investment, for agricultural activity, or for monopoly. Personal and business assets and other means of credit at reasonable terms must be utilized when feasible.

ECONOMIC INJURY DISASTER LOANS: (described in Disaster Relief section).

PHYSICAL DISASTER LOANS: (described in Disaster Relief section).

LEASE GUARANTEES: This program enables small businesses to obtain leases more easily by guaranteeing the rent payments under such leases. The maximum amount of aggregate rental under one lease that can be guaranteed is $2,500,000.

PROCUREMENT ASSISTANCE: Assistance includes (1) application of small business set-asides (restrictions of bidding/award to small businesses only); (2) review and analysis of small firms' capacity and credit when challenged by contracting officers, and, as appropriate, certifying the competence of such firms: (3) consultation and advice for small firms requesting assistance on Government procurement on sale matters; and (4) assistance in specific contract administration problems.

BUSINESS

MINORITY BUSINESS DEVELOPMENT: (described in Civil Rights section).

MANAGEMENT ASSISTANCE: SBA services in this area include (1) workshops for prospective small business owners; (2) management counseling for non-borrowers, including SCORE (Service Corps of Retired Executives) and ACE (Active Corps of Executives), and other volunteer groups; (3) management courses, conferences and clinics; (4) publications to assist in management and in the application of new technology; and (5) special business ownership training, in cooperation with the Veterans Administration for veterans (see Veterans section for further information).

ELIGIBILITY: A small business (prospective or existing) is generally defined as one that is independently owned and operated, and which is not dominant in its field. For manufacturers, average employment should not be over 250; for wholesalers, annual sales should not be over $5,000,000; while for retail and service concerns, revenue should not be over $1,000,000. Other specific criteria may be obtained from any SBA office.

Not eligible for small business loans or economic opportunity loans are gambling establishments, communications media, non-profit enterprises, or speculators in property, lending, or investment enterprises. Businesses seeking to finance real property which is held for sale or investment are also ineligible.

Eligible for economic opportunity loans are persons who either have low incomes or who, due to social or economic disadvantage, have been denied the opportunity to acquire adequate and reasonably-priced business financing through normal channels.

Small businesses that have suffered as a result of Federally-owned projects are eligible to apply for displaced business loans.

In some cases, members of community groups, as well as actual and potential small businesspersons are eligible for management assistance.

HOW TO APPLY: For loans, applications should be filed in the SBA field office serving the territory in which the applicant's business is located. When a participating bank (for instance, in the case of guaranteed/insured loans) is in another area, applications may be accepted and processed by the field office serving that territory, provided that there is mutual agreement between the two field offices involved.

Form lease guarantees, the lessor should file his part of the application (SBA For 800-A, Part I) with a private insurer or directly with the SBA. Required supporting information is listed on the form.

For procurement or management assistance, forms are available from SBA offices (Assistance to small businesses in the procurement of military contracts is available from the Defense Department. Apply to the Director, Small Business and Economic Utilization Policy, Room 3D777, the Pentagon, Washington, D.C. 20301).

FOR MORE INFORMATION: Small Business Administration
1441 L Street NW
Washington, D.C. 20416

RELATED PROGRAMS: Business Services and Information
Housing Rehabilitation
Minority Enterprise
Property Improvement Loan Insurance

LOANS FOR BUSINESS AND DEVELOPMENT COMPANIES

PROGRAM: This program seeks to encourage private investment by providing low-interest, long-term loans to help businesses expand or establish plants in redevelopment areas where adequate financing cannot be obtained from private sources.

Business development loans up to 65 per cent of the cost of fixed assets (a local development corporation or state agency usually participates to the extent of 5 per cent, with at least 10 per cent required to come from the applicant's equity and the balance from a conventional commercial lender) may be used for the acquisition of such assets only (i.e., land, building, machinery and equipment, including land preparation and building rehabilitation).

In some special cases, the Government can provide Federal guarantees of up to 90 per cent of the unpaid balance of working capital loans obtained from private lenders. Such guaranteed loans may not be used for the acquisition of fixed assets. Furthermore, loans can be guaranteed only for borrowers in the direct loan program.

ELIGIBILITY: Any individual, private or public corporation, or Indian tribe, provided that the project to be funded is physically situated in an area designated as eligible at the time the application is filed.

Neither business development loans nor working capital guarantees will be extended to applicants who (1) have, within the previous three years, relocated any or all of their facilities to another city or state; (2) contemplate relocating part or all of their existing facilities with a resultant loss of employment at such facilities; and (3) produce a product or service for which there is a sustained and prolonged excess of supply over demand.

No financial assistance will be given to projects primarily engaged in the dissemination of news (e.g., newspapers, magazines, radio and television broadcasting, or in an activity violating local or state law).

HOW TO APPLY: A prospective applicant should contact the Commerce Department's regional office serving the state in which the project is to be located. An economic development representative will then be assigned to the project. With the representative's concurrence, a pre-application conference will be scheduled with the professional staff of the regional office. At this conference, the applicant will be provided with all necessary forms and detailed information relating to supporting documentation.

NOTE: *These loans are not the nickel and dime variety, with the range extending from $120,000 to $5,590,000 and the average just over $1,300,000.*

FOR MORE INFORMATION: Office of Business Development
Economic Development Administration
Department of Commerce
Washington, D.C. 20230

RELATED PROGRAMS: Minority Business Development
Small Business Services

CRIME INSURANCE

PROGRAM: It's bad enough to be robbed or have your business or home burglarized, but it's much worse if you don't have insurance to cover the losses. Unfortunately the price for adequate crime insurance in many areas often has been extremely high.

To bring these costs down, Uncle Sam has gone into the insurance business himself. The Federal Insurance Administration (FIA) sells burglary and robbery policies, through insurance agents and brokers, to businesses and residents of homes and apartments in states where it has been ruled that there is a critical and continuing shortage of private crime insurance available at moderate rates.

Commercial policies protect separately against loss from burglary and robbery and provide coverages up to $15,000 on a per occurrence basis. Residential policies are combination burglary-robbery plans offering up to $5,000 coverage. Both commercial and residential policies are subject to deductibles.

ELIGIBILITY: Lists of designated states may be obtained from any insurance agent, broker, or from the servicing companies designated as follows: Aetna Casualty & Surety Co. (Connecticut, District of Columbia, Massachusetts, Missouri, New York and Ohio), Insurance Company of North America (Illinois, Maryland and Pennsylvania) and American Universal Insurance Co. (Rhode Island).

The applicant, in addition to paying the specified premium, must have protective equipment which meets FIA standards. Protective devices are not currently required for premises insured against loss from robbery only. Commerical premiums vary according to type of business and gross receipts, and both commerical and residential premiums reflect the crime rate of the area in which the premises are located.

HOW TO APPLY: Eligible applicants must complete the Application Form (and any amendatory endorsements which may be in use) provided by local insurance agents, brokers, or the servicing companies (HUD Forms 1621, 1621a, 1631, or 1631a).

FOR MORE INFORMATION: Federal Insurance Administration
Department of Housing and Urban Development
Washington, D.C. 20410

RELATED PROGRAMS: Urban Property Insurance

BUSINESS SERVICES AND INFORMATION

PROGRAM: The Bureau of Domestic Commerce handles inquiries (950,000 in fiscal year 1971) and distributes information regarding Commerce Department products and services.

General areas of service include guidance on pending legislation and regulations; data and assistance concerning government procurement; studies analyzing growth and outlook for specific industries; statistical data and publications; narrative outlook analyses for U.S. industrial activity; foreign trade information; information on technical developments and their impact on industry and regional growth; information on special conferences and on trade and professional associations; and assistance in supply/maintenance problems in times of emergency.

ELIGIBILITY: Any business, public official, civic organization or private citizen may apply.

HOW TO APPLY: In person, by letter or by telephone.

FOR MORE INFORMATION: Bureau of Domestic Commerce
Department of Commerce
Washington, D.C. 20230

RELATED PROGRAMS: Census Services
International Commercial Information
Small Business Services

DOING BUSINESS WITH THE FEDERAL GOVERNMENT

PROGRAM: Uncle Sam means business.

Business, that is, to the numerous companies that help fill the many and varied needs of the Federal Government each year.

If you'd like to learn how to compete for a piece of the action, the General Services Administration stands ready to help you. The GSA provides information and counseling to assist business firms, especially small and minority businesses, in developing Government market potential for their products and services, in obtaining contracting opportunities, and in purchasing surplus property.

Examples of business opportunities within the Federal Government include supplying any of the thousands of items offered for sale on military exchanges (concession contracts ranging from barbershops to bowling alleys are also available on military bases), repairing or renovating Government facilities, and filling Federal supply and service needs.

ELIGIBILITY: Any business concern is eligible.

HOW TO APPLY: Contact the nearest GSA Business Service Center by letter, telephone, or in person. The appropriate form (depending on whether the individual or business concern wishes to buy or sell its goods and/or services) will then be given for completion.

FOR MORE INFORMATION: Business Services Office
General Services Administration
Washington, D.C. 20405

RELATED PROGRAMS: Minority Business Enterprise
Small Business Services

PATENTS AND TRADEMARKS

PROGRAM: Do you think you've built a better mouse trap? Before the world starts its proverbial path to your door, you would be well advised to beat your own path, literally or figuratively, to the door of the Patent Office.

If the Patent Office approves your application for a patent, you or your assignee will then have the sole right to manufacture your mouse trap for 17 years, after which it will enter the public domain.

Since it is possible and legal to use the technical information contained in a patent in different ways, the Patent Office maintains a public search center at its headquarters at 2021 Jefferson Davis Highway, Arlington, Virginia. Housed there is the world's largest collection of applied technical information, including 3,500,000 U.S. patents and related documents and several million foreign patents. The patents are arranged by classes and subclasses for searching, which may be done on weekdays from 8 a.m. to 8 p.m. without charge.

The Patent Office also sells copies of patents (an average of 22,000 a *day*) at $.50 each. Copies of trademarks are also available for a fee, or may be examined at the search center.

ELIGIBILITY: Everyone is eligible.

HOW TO APPLY: Letter or personal inquiry to the Patent Office Headquarters, 2021 Jefferson Davis Highway, Arlington, Virginia.

FOR MORE INFORMATION: U.S. Patent Office
Department of Commerce
Washington, D.C. 20231

RELATED PROGRAMS: Licensing of AEC Patents
Technical Information

LICENSING OF AEC PATENTS

PROGRAM: To encourage widespread utilization of inventions covered by Atomic Energy Commission patents, the AEC grants nonexclusive, royalty-free, revocable licenses on patents owned by it. The licenses are granted on request to U.S. citizens and corporations on over 4,500 AEC-owned U.S. patents. Similar licenses on over 3,400 AEC-owned foreign patents may be accorded to U.S. citizens and corporations, and to others under terms and conditions which depend on the particular situation.

Abstracts of most AEC-owned patents are published in "Nuclear Science Abstracts," a journal published by AEC and sold by the Government Printing Office. Abstracts of current acquisitions may be obtained without charge from the AEC Division of Public Information. Copies of patents may also be obtained for $.50 each from the Patent Office in Washington.

ELIGIBILITY: Individuals, firms, or corporations, domestic and foreign, may apply.

HOW TO APPLY: By letter to the Assistant General Counsel for Patents, U.S. Atomic Energy Commission, Washington, D.C. 20545, identifying the patent by number, together with information as to (1) the nature and type of the company's (or individual's) business; (2) the purpose for which the license is desired, together with a brief statement on the plan to achieve that purpose; (3) the geographical areas in which the company will practice the invention; (4) the company's willingness to render periodic reports on the use of the licensed subject matter; and (5) the company's status as a small business firm, minority business, or other.

FOR MORE INFORMATION: Assistant General Counsel for U.S. Patents
U. S. Atomic Energy Commission
Washington, D.C. 20545

RELATED PROGRAMS: Nuclear Science Information
Patents and Trademarks

TECHNICAL INFORMATION

PROGRAMS: The Departments of Commerce and Labor make available a wide variety of technical information to the general public. Some of the data is free and available for the asking, while other information may be purchased.

In the Department of Commerce, such information is available from the Social and Economic Statistics Administration, the National Bureau of Standards, and the National Technical Information Service.

The Social and Economic Statistics Administration, in addition to providing census information (see Information section), prepares and distributes measures and analyses relating to the national economy. This information generally appears in the monthly publication "Survey of Current Business" and its weekly supplements. A one-year subscription, including supplements, is $9.00; a single issue is $1.00. Subscriptions are available from the Superintendent of Documents, U.S. Government Printing Office, Washington, D.C. 20402.

Technical information from the National Bureau of Standards includes reference data and materials pertaining to standards, calibrations and testing, and weights and measures services. Standard reference data is on the chemical and physical properties of materials, while standard reference materials can be used in quality control, determination of performance characteristics, and scientific research. The NBS provides, on a fee basis, calibrations of standards and measuring devices that require a high degree of accuracy. Weights and measures services include publications, special studies, legal and technical assistance, and technical training.

The National Technical Information Service (NTIS) is responsible for the collection, cataloging, announcement and public sale of Federally-sponsored technical information, including reports, magnetic tapes, microform and data tabulations. Announcement services, published biweekly, are designed to keep users abreast of new information in major subject matter fields. The services include Government Reports Announcements, Government Reports Topical Announcements, Government Reports Index, and a Fast Announcement Service.

NTIS has 688,000 scientific, technical, and engineering reports available in either paper copy or microfiche form. For a fee, the Service will provide computer-generated bibliographic searches for its users. Additionally , under a new program, the NTIS catalogs and indexes summary statistical data of the Department of Commerce.

The Department of Labor distributes technical information chiefly from its Bureau of Labor Statistics, which provides data in the following areas: manpower and employment, prices and cost of living, productivity and technology, wages and industrial relations, and economic research.

Manpower and employment data includes employment and unemployment analysis on the current economic status of workers, labor force studies, and occupational employment statistics, including employment outlook, nature of the work, earnings, working conditions, and qualifications.

Prices and cost of living data includes consumer and wholesale price indexes. As the basis for most estimates of changes in real earnings, the consumer price index figures significantly in wage adjustments and collective bargaining. Other cost of living data includes standard budgets for a city worker's family and a retired couple at three levels of living. These are helpful in budget planning, assessment of welfare needs and setting of fees. In addition, a Consumer Expenditure Survey provides information on changes in spending patterns, income, and assets.

Productivity and technology data includes private economy and sector productivity measurements, labor requirement studies, studies of the impact of technology on manpower, and economic growth studies providing long-range projections for the U.S. economy and explaining inter-industry relationships.

Wages and industrial relations data includes wage studies for selected occupations in about 180 areas, compensation studies made for nonagricultural employment biennially (with selected industries studies in the intervening years), wage trend studies, and industrial relations studies providing collective bargaining agreement analysis, information on work stoppages, and labor union directories.

Economic research data includes projections, under alternative assumptions, of the rate and patterns of growth in the economy, projections of inter-industry sales and purchases based on anticipated changes in technology, estimates of the demand for labor in an 82-sector breakdown of the economy, assessments of current economic conditions and analysis of short-run economic developments, and specialized research in socioeconomic conditions.

ELIGIBILITY: Everyone is eligible to receive or purchase, depending on the service, any of the technical information described above.

HOW TO APPLY: Information on the economic data available from the Social and Economic Statistics Administration may be obtained by contacting the nearest Department of Commerce Field Office.

For calibrations, submit a purchase order to the Office of Measurement Services or appropriate technical division, National Bureau of Standards, Department of Commerce, Washington, D.C. 20234 *or* to Office of Management Services or appropriate technical division, National Bureau of Standards, Department of Commerce, Boulder, Colorado 80302.

For reference data on standards, submit a purchase order to the Superintendent of Documents, U. S. Government Printing Office, Washington, D.C. 20402, while for reference materials on standards, the order should be sent to the Office of Standard Reference Materials, National Bureau of Standards, Washington, D. C. 20234.

To request weights and measures services, send a letter to Chief, Office of Weights and Measures, Institute for Applied Technology, Washington, D.C. 20234.

For National Technical Information Services, write NTIS, 5285 Port Royal Road, Springfield, Virginia 22151.

Requests for data or assistance in any of the areas covered by the Bureau of Labor Statistics may be obtained by writing to the nearest Regional Office.

FOR MORE INFORMATION: (particular division)
Department of Commerce
Washington, D.C. 20230

or

Bureau of Labor Statistics
Department of Labor
Washington, D.C. 20212

RELATED PROGRAMS: Business Services and Information
Census Information
Science Information and Exchange

INTERNATIONAL COMMERCIAL INFORMATION

PROGRAM: Firms desiring to initiate or expand their international markets may obtain information from the Commerce Department on overseas opportunities, foreign economics, trade openings abroad, government financial aid to exporters, as well as information on export quotas and tariffs. The Bureau provides guidance to U.S. businesses through the use of foreign marketing journals and statistical reports. Information and assistance in attracting private foreign investment to the United States are also available.

ELIGIBILITY: No restrictions.

HOW TO APPLY: In person, or by letter or telephone to the local Department of Commerce field office.

FOR MORE INFORMATION: Bureau of International Commerce
Department of Commerce
Washington, D.C. 20230

RELATED PROGRAMS: Business Services and Information
Export Services

LABOR-MANAGEMENT RELATIONS SERVICES

PROGRAM: The Department of Labor, through its Labor-Management Services Administration, provides assistance including consultations and publications, in developing sound labor-management relations and in resolving problems between the two groups. This agency also seeks to protect the interests of employees affected by projects authorized under the Urban Mass Transportation Act, the High-Speed Ground Transportation Act, and the Rail Passenger Service Act of 1970.

ELIGIBILITY: Assistance is available to all groups and individuals in the public and private sectors.

HOW TO APPLY: Oral or written communication with the office below.

FOR MORE INFORMATION: Office of Labor-Management Relations Services
Department of Labor
14th and Constitution Avenue NW
Washington, D.C. 20210

RELATED PROGRAMS: None

FISHERY SERVICES

PROGRAMS: The National Marine Fisheries Service, a division of the National Oceanic and Atmospheric Administration, provides a variety of assistance to the commercial fishing industry, including both direct and mortgage insurance loans to upgrade fishing vessels and gear, insurance against seizure of vessels, and fishery publications.

In order to obtain a direct loan, evidence must be supplied that the credit applied for is not otherwise available on reasonable terms. No loan can be made for any phase of a shore operation, for a nonmaritime lien, for repair or purchase of a vessel or gear not offered as collateral, or for a new business venture controlled by persons not engaged in commercial fishing. For purchase or construction of a vessel, a determination must be made that operation will not cause economic hardship or injury to efficient vessel operators already in that fishery.

Mortgage insurance, up to 75 per cent of the actual vessel cost, is available to lenders providing funds for construction, reconstruction or reconditioning of fishing vessels.

The Fishermen's Protective Fund provides for the reimbursement of losses and costs incurred as a result of the seizure of a U.S. commercial fishing vessel on the basis of rights or claims not recognized by the United States, whether in territorial waters or on the high seas. The vessel must be documented or certified under American laws.

(Fines, license fees, registration fees, and other direct costs paid to secure prompt release of a vessel and crew are not reimbursable under this program, but, rather, through the Secretary of State. Contact the Office of the Legal Adviser, Department of State, Washington, D.C. 20250. No prior registration or payment of premiums is necessary to qualify for such reimbursement.)

Publications of interest to the fishing industry include both statistical and market news reports and quarterly situation and outlook analyses. The statistical and market news features data on harvesting fish resources, production of processed fishery products, receipts, wholesale prices, and foreign trade information. The situation and outlook reports cover economic conditions in relation to fresh fish, shellfish, and industrial fishery. Publications and assistance are also available to persons in the fishing industry who have an interest in forming cooperatives.

ELIGIBILITY: To be eligible for a direct loan, the applicant must be a U.S. citizen or national residing in the United States who (1) owns, operates, or will own a commercial fishing vessel or gear used, or to be used, directly in conducting fishing operations; and (2) demonstrates the ability, experience, resources and other qualifications necessary for successful operation. Fishing cooperatives are also eligible to apply for direct loans.

For the mortgage insurance program, the person receiving the insurance must be approved by the Secretary of Commerce in relation to ability, experience, financial resources and other qualifications necessary for adequate operation and maintenance. The mortgagee must also receive approval.

To be eligible for insurance against seizure, the only requirements are U.S. citizenship and being the owner or charterer of a fishing vessel documented as such by the United States.

There are no restrictions on the receiving of fishery publications.

HOW TO APPLY: Requests for applications for financial assistance or insurance should be directed to the Chief, Financial Assistance Division, National Marine Fisheries Service (address below). The insurance and mortgage insurance programs require a filing fee to be submitted with the application.

Applications for fishery publications may be made to any office of the National Marine Fisheries Service.

FOR MORE INFORMATION: National Marine Fisheries Service
1801 North Moore Street
Arlington, Virginia 22209

RELATED PROGRAMS: Freshwater Fishery Information
Technical Information

SHIPS—SALES AND MORTGAGE INSURANCE

PROGRAMS: If you've always wanted to own your own ship, perhaps Uncle Sam can help you out. Every year the Government sells, by competitive bid, merchant ships which have become surplus to Federal needs. After sale, a ship must be used for a non-transportation use, such as for a pier, warehouse, oil drilling platform or crane platform, or for dismantling purposes.

Besides selling its own ships, the Government provides mortgage insurance to owners of private vessels which are designed for research or for commercial use (a) in coastwide or intercoastal trade; (b) on the Great Lakes or on bays, sounds, rivers, harbors, or inland lakes of the United States; (c) in foreign trade; (d) in fishing trade, or floating drydocks. The vessel must not be a towboat, barge, scow, lighter, car float, canal boat or tank vessel of less than 200 gross tons.

ELIGIBILITY: Anyone who has a need for a ship for either a non-transportation or dismantling purpose is eligible to receive an invitation to bid.

Mortgage insurance is available to any U.S. citizen with the ability, experience, financial resources, and other qualifications necessary for the adequate operation and maintenance of the mortgaged property. The bank providing the loan must also be approved by the Maritime Administration.

HOW TO APPLY: Prospective shipbuyers should write to the Maritime Administration for an invitation to bid. Applicants for mortgage insurance should file loan form MA163 through a Regional Director of the Maritime Administration. The application must be approved in principle prior to the keel-laying of a vessel to be constructed or prior to the commencement of work on a vessel to be reconstructed or reconditioned.

FOR MORE INFORMATION: Maritime Administration
Department of Commerce
Washington, D.C. 20235

RELATED PROGRAMS: Investigation of Shipping Complaints

EXPORT SERVICES

PROGRAMS: The Bureau of International Commerce provides information and advisory services to persons and businesses interested in export trade. Assistance ranges from interpreting export control regulations and policies regarding licensing to helping with display and sales promotion (trade centers, business information centers and fairs) and representing U.S. firms before government agencies at home and abroad.

The Bureau also supplies information on trade statistics, foreign tariffs and customs regulations, as well as general advice and counseling on foreign trade. It also provides assistance in securing rapid handling of export applications when priority action is warranted.

ELIGIBILITY: Any person, firm, organization, or branch of government needing information or assistance in any of the broad areas listed above.

HOW TO APPLY: In person, or by letter or telephone to any local Department of Commerce field office.

FOR MORE INFORMATION: Bureau of International Commerce
Department of Commerce
Washington, D.C. 20230

RELATED PROGRAMS: Business Services and Information
International Commercial Information

CHAPTER 5

Farming

When one agricultural program (Price Supports) alone distributes $734,716,000 in direct payments and $1,769,588,000 in loans in just one year (1971), it's not too hard to understand why benefits to farmers have become some of the most controversial (and often misunderstood) of all Government programs.

Supporters claim that the benefits are necessary incentives for continued agricultural production. Critics retort that the programs are excessive and represent unnecessary concessions to powerful legislators and special interest groups.

You can't tell the players without a scorecard, and you can't make an intelligent evaluation of farm benefits without understanding them. This chapter describes the programs open to individual farmers, ranging from the massive system of price supports to little-known benefits such as low cost housing loans to farm laborers.

So, if you're not a farmer, you probably won't obtain any material gain from this chapter, but we hope that you read it anyway for a basic understanding of these hotly-debated programs.

PRICE SUPPORTS

PROGRAMS: The Agricultural Stabilization and Conservation Service (ASCS) provides support loans and purchases to producers of a variety of crops, including feed grains, wheat, rice, beans, honey, cotton, dairy products, peanuts, tobacco, seeds, and plants.

Price support loans are "nonrecourse," which means that producers do not have to make good any decline in the market price of the commodity they have put up as collateral. If market prices rise above support, producers can pay off their loan and market their commodity, while if market prices fail to rise above support prices, producers can pay off the loan completely through forfeiture of the collateral.

In conjunction with the program of price support loans to commodity producers, the ASCS also provides loans for the financing of needed storage facilities and drying equipment.

ELIGIBILITY: Any person, who, as owner, landlord, tenant, or sharecropper, is entitled to share in crops on a farm having a history of producing the specified commodities, is eligible for price supports.

For storage and equipment loans, such person must produce one or more of the following commodities: barley, corn, grain sorghum, oats, rye, wheat, soybeans, sunflower seed, rice, dry edible beans, flaxseed, peanuts, and baled hay for emergency use.

HOW TO APPLY: To apply for price supports, the farmer should present warehouse receipts to the county office or the appropriate cooperative association. If he stores the commodities on his farm, the farmer should inform the county office that he wants a loan.

Loans are available, depending on the commodity, for periods of six to eight months after harvest. Purchases from producers are made at the time of loan maturity for the crop.

To apply for a loan for storage facilities or drying equipment, the producer must file Form CCC 185 in the county office. The form must indicate production, name of vendor from whom the facility will be purchased, and the cost of the proposed installation. Paid receipts must also be furnished. Applications must be filed not later than 30 days after delivery of the structure or equipment to the farm.

FOR MORE INFORMATION: Agricultural Stabilization and
Conservation Service
Department of Agriculture
Washington, D.C. 20250

RELATED PROGRAMS: Commodity Payments
                                     Export Payments

COMMODITY PAYMENTS

PROGRAMS: Farmers who choose *not* to produce part of their cotton, feed grain, sugar, or wheat crops may receive compensation from the Agricultural Stabilization and Conservation Service. Producers of wool and mohair also are eligible to receive supporting payments from the Agricultural Stabilization and Conservation Service.

Producers of cotton, feed grain, or wheat can earn payments by setting aside an acreage from crop production equal to a specified percentage of the base while maintaining the farm's conserving base. Producers of sugar must not harvest an acreage in excess of the proportionate share established for their farms.

ELIGIBILITY: Any person who as owner, landlord, tenant, or sharecropper on a farm that has a history of producing cotton, feed grain, or wheat is eligible to apply for payments for those commodities.

Sugar beet and sugar cane producers must also agree to comply with specified wage and labor requirements.

Persons who own sheep, lambs or goats for 30 days or more, and sell, respectively, shorn wool, unshorn lambs, or mohair are eligible for payments.

HOW TO APPLY: Farmers should complete the appropriate forms at the local ASCS county office. Wool and mohair producers must turn in a bill of sale with their applications.

NOTE: *Did you ever wonder why payments to wealthy farmers who do not produce certain commodities are often called "subsidies," while welfare payments to the poor are just as often called "handouts?"*

FOR MORE INFORMATION: Agricultural Stabilization and
                                             Conservation Service
                                             Department of Agriculture
                                             Washington, D.C. 20250

RELATED PROGRAMS: Export Payments
                                     Price Supports

EXPORT PAYMENTS

PROGRAMS: Exporters of agricultural products or grains (wheat, flour, rice, or tobacco) may receive subsidies to keep their products competitive in world markets.

ELIGIBILITY: Agricultural and grain exporters. Grain may only be exported to eligible destinations.

HOW TO APPLY: Representative agricultural groups may request assistance when they encounter a loss on export markets. The individual agricultural exporter must submit bids on the quantity of the product to be exported. Grain exporters must submit a written statement of financial responsibility and evidence of being a bona fide exporter to the Export Marketing Service.

FOR MORE INFORMATION: Marketing Services
Consumer and Marketing Service
Department of Agriculture
Washington, D.C. 20250

or

Assistant Sales Manager (Commodity Exports)
Export Marketing Service
Department of Agriculture
Washington, D.C. 20250

RELATED PROGRAMS: Export Information

FARM LOANS

PROGRAMS: The Farmers Home Administration (FHA) provides loans to help farmers meet the costs of farm operation and/or ownership.

ELIGIBILITY: Applicants for either type of loan must be (a) U.S. citizens of legal age; (b) of good character; (c) possess the necessary experience, training and ability to be successful; and (d) unable to obtain sufficient credit elsewhere on reasonable terms. Applicants for farm operating loans must also agree to operate nothing larger than a family farm.

HOW TO APPLY: File FHA Form 410-1, "Application for FHA Services," at the local county office of the Farmers Home Administration.

FOR MORE INFORMATION: Farmers Home Administration
Department of Agriculture
Washington, D.C. 20250

NOTE: *These loans can be used for a wide variety of purposes including forestry, recreational facilities and other non-farm enterprises operated on the farm.*

RELATED PROGRAMS: Property Improvement Loan Insurance
Veterans Business and Farm Loans

LOAN INSURANCE FOR CONSTRUCTION OF NONRESIDENTIAL FARM STRUCTURES

PROGRAM: To facilitate financing for the construction of proposed nonresidential farm structures, the Federal Housing Administration (FHA) insures loans of $5,000 or less. The financing charge is at an annual rate of 8.83 to 10.57 per cent (5.86 to 6.25 per cent if the term of the loan exceeds seven years and 32 days).

ELIGIBILITY: Eligible borrowers include the owner of the property to be improved or a lessee having a lease extending at least six months beyond maturity of the loan.

HOW TO APPLY: Apply directly to an FHA-insured lender.

FOR MORE INFORMATION: Assistant Commissioner for
Property Improvement
Housing Production and Mortgage Credit/FHA
Department of Housing and
Urban Development
Washington, D.C. 20410

RELATED PROGRAMS: Farm Loans
Property Improvement Loan Insurance

FARM LABOR HOUSING LOANS

PROGRAM: The Farmers Home Administration makes available guaranteed and insured loans to assist farmers in providing decent, safe and sanitary low-rent housing for domestic farm laborers.

Loans may be used for construction, repair or purchase of housing; for acquiring the necessary land for the housing and making improvements on it; and for developing related facilities, such as central cooking and dining facilities. Housing must be practical and be constructed economically.

ELIGIBILITY: Farmers and associations of farmers are eligible to apply for loans.

HOW TO APPLY: An indefinite moratorium has been placed on this and other subsidized housing programs. Any FHA office will be able to supply the latest information on the status of the moratorium.

FOR MORE INFORMATION: Farmers Home Administration
Department of Agriculture
Washington, D.C. 20250

RELATED PROGRAMS: Low to Moderate Income Housing Loans
Mortgage Insurance (Homes in Outlying Areas)
Rural Rental Housing Loans

FARM RECREATIONAL FACILITY LOANS

PROGRAM: Would you like to put some more fun into your farm? If you are willing to turn part or all of it into an outdoor recreational facility, you may be eligible to receive a loan from the Department of Agriculture.

The Farmers Home Administration makes the loans, which farmers and ranch owners or tenants may use to finance the following kinds of outdoor recreational enterprises: camp grounds, riding stables, swimming facilities, tennis courts, shooting preserves, lakes and ponds for boating and fishing, docks, nature trails, hunting facilities, winter sports areas, and guest lodging.

The loan funds, which are scheduled for repayment over 40 years, may be used to (1) develop land and water resources; (2) repair and construct buildings; (3) purchase land, equipment, livestock and related recreational items; and (4) pay necessary operating expenses.

ELIGIBILITY: Applicants must be farmers who are U.S. citizens of legal age and good character. They must have adequate experience or training in the proposed recreational enterprise, but must be unable to obtain adequate credit from other sources at reasonable terms. They must also agree to refinance the balance due on loans as soon as they are able to obtain adequate credit at reasonable terms from another lender.

HOW TO APPLY: File form FHA 410-1, "Application for FHA Services," at the local county office of the Farmers Home Administration.

FOR MORE INFORMATION: Farmers Home Administration
Department of Agriculture
Washington, D.C. 20250

RELATED PROGRAMS: Farm Pond Stocking

FARM POND STOCKING

PROGRAM: Would you like to have your farm pond filled with fish? If you're willing to allow controlled public fishing, the Bureau of Sport Fisheries and Wildlife may stock your pond for you.

Fish are not available for ponds which are less than one-quarter acre in size, subject to any form of commercialization, or apparently biologically incapable of sustaining fish life. Trout and channel catfish are only stocked once.

ELIGIBILITY: Individuals, organizations and municipalities owning suitable ponds are eligible to receive fish. In general, eligible individually-owned ponds are those created with technical and financial assistance from the Department of Agriculture.

Each applicant is "urged to permit controlled public fishing, in accordance with all applicable laws and regulations" in stocked ponds.

HOW TO APPLY: Obtain application form 3-1688 from the Bureau's Washington or regional offices and return to the appropriate regional office on completion.

FOR MORE INFORMATION: Bureau of Sport Fisheries and Wildlife
Department of the Interior
Washington, D.C. 20240

RELATED PROGRAMS: Farm Recreational Facility Loans
Rural Environmental Assistance

CROP INSURANCE

PROGRAM: The Department of Agriculture offers all-risk crop insurance to individual farmers as protection against drought, freezes, insects, and other natural causes of disastrous crop losses.

ELIGIBILITY: Any owner or operator of farmland who has an insurable interest in a crop in a county where insurance is offered for that crop (insurance is available in over 1,400 agricultural counties in 39 states) is eligible, unless the land is not classified for insurance purposes.

HOW TO APPLY: Form FCI-12, "Application for Federal Crop Insurance for 1972 and Succeeding Crop Years," must be filed with a Federal Crop Insurance Corporation representative.

FOR MORE INFORMATION: Federal Crop Insurance Corporation
Department of Agriculture
Washington, D.C. 20250

RELATED PROGRAMS: Emergency Loans
Flood Insurance

NATIONAL AGRICULTURAL LIBRARY

PROGRAM: The National Agricultural Library is the national resource for information on agriculture and related subjects. Materials are available in over 50 different languages.

ELIGIBILITY: Anyone can use the Library's services. Publications are available through interlibrary loan or photoreproduction.

HOW TO APPLY: Apply by letter to:
Division of Lending

or

Division of Reference
National Agricultural Library
Beltsville, Maryland 20705

RELATED PROGRAMS: Agricultural Information

AGRICULTURAL INFORMATION

PROGRAMS: Agricultural information is available from many agencies of the Department of Agriculture.

The Office of Information publishes bulletins and leaflets on a variety of subjects of interest to farmers, suburbanites, homemakers and consumers. The Office also maintains a central library of newstype color and black/white photos obtained in connection with USDA work. In addition, the Office of Information provides slide sets, filmstrips, motion pictures and exhibits on agricultural and home economics subjects.

Information on agricultural topics may also be obtained from the following agencies of the Department of Agriculture: Agricultural Research Service; Agricultural Marketing Service (market news on major agricultural commodities); Economic Research Service; and the Statistical Reporting Service (crop and livestock estimates).

ELIGIBILITY: Anyone may receive information.

HOW TO APPLY: Write to:
(particular agency)
Department of Agriculture
Washington, D.C. 20250

RELATED PROGRAMS: National Agricultural Library

CHAPTER 6

Environment

There have been many "movements" in the last decade. Civil Rights. Women's Liberation. Student Power. And numerous others, each with its own ideology, slogans and intensity.

But the one movement that has probably attracted the most diversified following has been the battle to protect our natural resources and prevent the continued despoiling of our environment.

As more legislators and government leaders have become sensitive to environmental issues, there has been a corresponding growth in the number of related Federal programs, a growth which many hope will accelerate in the coming years.

In this section, you will find programs that provide information about pesticides, wildlife, mineral deposits and our old friend, the weather. You will learn that some public lands may be purchased from the Government and that, under certain conditions, persons may be allowed free use of some timber products. If you are a farmer or rancher, you should note the various programs designed to encourage the adoption of conservation practices.

Something for everyone, we hope.

Because the environment is everyone's business.

PESTICIDE INFORMATION

PROGRAMS: Concerned about the effects of pesticides? The Federal Government has two agencies that may be able to provide you with helpful information.

The Environmental Protection Agency (Office of Pesticides Programs) provides information concerning exposure to and the toxic effects of pesticides and other chemicals introduced into man's environment. A range of publications and specialized information services are available free or for purchase.

The Bureau of Sport Fisheries and Wildlife, Department of the Interior, conducts a monitoring and technical assistance program on pesticide-fish-wildlife ecology.

ELIGIBILITY: All persons are eligible for information.

HOW TO APPLY: Contact:
Environmental Protection Agency
Pesticides Programs
Division of Community Studies
4770 Buford Highway
Building 29
Chamblee, Georgia 30341

or

Bureau of Sport Fisheries and Wildlife
Department of the Interior
Washington, D.C. 20240

RELATED PROGRAMS: Payments for Pesticide Damage
Wildlife Research Information

PAYMENTS FOR PESTICIDE DAMAGE

PROGRAM: Dairy farmers and beekeepers who suffer losses as a result of the use of pesticides may have the "sting" alleviated by receiving compensation from the Agricultural Stabilization and Conservation Service.

ELIGIBILITY: A dairy farmer's milk or a dairy manufacturer's product must have been removed from the market by a public agency or a milk handler because of pesticide residue. No payments will be made for removals resulting from willful failure to follow procedures for the pesticide as prescribed by the Federal Government.

A beekeeper must establish that he suffered, through no fault of his own, a loss of bees as a result of the use of pesticides near or adjacent to his apiary; that if he used pesticides, they in no way contributed to the loss; and that if he had advance notice that pesticides were going to be used near his apiary, he took reasonable steps to protect his bees.

No payments may be made to beekeepers whose bees die as a result of pesticides which have not been registered and approved for use by the Federal Government.

HOW TO APPLY: Forms should be filed with the local county Agricultural Stabilization and Conservation Service office. Dairy farmers and manufacturers should file Form ASCS-373, while beekeepers should file either Form ASCS 448 or 449. The dairy application deadline is August 31, 1973; beekeepers must file within a year of the loss.

FOR MORE INFORMATION: Agricultural Stabilization and
Conservation Service
Department of Agriculture
Washington, D.C. 20250

RELATED PROGRAMS: Pesticide Information

WEATHER FORECASTS AND WARNINGS

PROGRAM: Want to know what the weather is going to be?

The National Weather Service warns the general public of impending severe weather, issues routine weather forecasts up to 48 hours in advance, provides weather outlooks up to five days in advance, and also gives various weather summaries.

ELIGIBILITY: Everyone is eligible.

HOW TO APPLY: Send written requests to a regional office of the National Weather Service.

FOR MORE INFORMATION: National Weather Service
National Oceanic and
  Atmospheric Administration
8060 13th Street
Silver Spring, Maryland 20910

RELATED PROGRAMS: River and Flood Forecasts

RIVER AND FLOOD FORECASTS

PROGRAM: In the interests of public safety and the management and conservation of water resources, the National Weather Service provides forecasts of the water levels of the country's rivers. In the case of potential
floods, the warnings can save life and property. Data can be useful to state
and local governments, major industries and the general public.

ELIGIBILITY: Everyone is eligible to receive the forecasts.

HOW TO APPLY: Verbal or written requests to:
Office of Hydrology
National Weather Service
National Oceanic and Atmospheric Administration
8060 13th Street
Silver Spring, Maryland 20910

RELATED PROGRAMS: Flood Insurance
Soil and Water Services
Weather Forecasts and Warnings

WILDLIFE RESEARCH INFORMATION

PROGRAM: The Bureau of Sport Fisheries and Wildlife provides information on the following subjects: migratory game birds, upland wildlife, wildlife diseases and parasites, pesticide-wildlife relationships, wildlife damage control methods, environmental pollutant research, classification, distribution and life histories of wildlife species, and endangered species.

ELIGIBILITY: No requirements.

HOW TO APPLY: Send a letter to the headquarters or field offices of the Bureau of Sport Fisheries and Wildlife. Interested individuals may have their names placed on the mailing list for announcements of research reports.

FOR MORE INFORMATION: Division of Wildlife Research
Bureau of Sport Fisheries and Wildlife
Department of the Interior
Washington, D.C. 20240

RELATED PROGRAMS: Freshwater Fishery Information
Pesticides Information
Water Bank Program

FRESHWATER FISHERY INFORMATION

PROGRAM: The Bureau of Sport Fisheries and Wildlife compiles and distributes information needed for the protection and enhancement of freshwater fishery resources, both public and private. Studies concentrate on fish physiology and behavior, as influenced by usual or abnormal environmental variables. Many technical publications and reprints are available.

ELIGIBILITY: Anyone may apply.

HOW TO APPLY: By correspondence, telephone, or personal visit to Bureau laboratory or headquarters.

FOR MORE INFORMATION: Division of Fishery Research
Bureau of Sport Fisheries and Wildlife
Department of the Interior
Washington, D. C. 20240

RELATED PROGRAMS: Fishery Services
Pesticide Information
Wildlife Research Information

TIMBER SALES AND FREE USAGE

PROGRAMS: The Bureau of Land Management offers forest products, primarily sawtimber, to private citizens and domestic corporations at public auction or through negotiated sales.

The Bureau also permits, under certain conditions, free use of small quantities of some forest products.

ELIGIBILITY: The prospective purchaser of timber must be (a) a U.S. citizen; (b) a partnership of citizens; or (c) a corporation authorized to do business in the state where the timber is located. A bid deposit representing 10 per cent of the sale-approved value must be submitted.

Eligible for free use of timber are (a) bona fide settlers; (b) mining claimants; or (c) a non-profit organization or agency. Requirements vary by state.

HOW TO APPLY: Persons interested in buying timber may secure negotiated sales when the volume is less than 250,000 board feet and when no competition exists. Notices of all sales of over 250,000 board feet are sent to all interested bidders and advertised in local newspapers. Interested buyers who would like certain tracts of timber to be advertised for public auction may complete Form 5410 for submission to local, area or district managers of the Bureau of Land Management.

To apply for free use of timber, submit two copies of Form 5510, "Free Use Application and Permit," to the nearest BLM Land Office or to an official authorized to issue a permit.

FOR MORE INFORMATION: Division of Forestry
Bureau of Land Management
Department of the Interior
Washington, D.C. 20240

RELATED PROGRAMS: Mineral Services

SALE OF PUBLIC LANDS

PROGRAM: Uncle Sam might be willing to sell you some public land, providing that it is isolated, disconnected, too rough for cultivation, or more valuable under non-Federal ownership.

If you're still interested, you should also know that lands for sale under these criteria must be in a state served by a regional office of the Bureau of Land Management.

(It is also technically possible for individuals to acquire surplus Federal property to be used for low or moderate income housing. Contact the Office of New Community Development, Department of Housing and Urban Development, Washington, D.C. 20410 for more information.)

ELIGIBILITY: For purchase of an isolated tract, any citizen of the U. S. (or anyone who has declared intention of becoming a citizen) who is at least 21 years old is eligible. For a tract, the greater part of which is mountainous or too rough for cultivation, any person who owns contiguous land or has a valid entry on land adjoining the tract may apply.

An isolated or disconnected parcel may not exceed 1,520 acres. Adjacent landowners may file applications to buy not more than 760 acres of mountainous or rough tracts.

HOW TO APPLY: Petition for classification on Form 2400-7, and apply on Form 2710-1 to the land office having jurisdiction. There is a service charge of $25 and an additional $50 charge to help defray the costs of publication of the proposed land sale.

FOR MORE INFORMATION: Division of Lands and Realty
Bureau of Land Management
Department of the Interior
Washington, D.C. 20240

RELATED PROGRAMS: None

MINERAL SERVICES

PROGRAM: Did you ever feel the urge to do some mining? The Bureau of Land Management leases Federally-owned mineral deposits to interested parties who then have the right to extract or remove the minerals for which the lease is issued.

The Bureau also sells mineral materials from Federally-owned lands. Sales must not be for less than the appraisal price though, so don't expect bottom-of-the-barrel prices.

For those persons interested in learning about minerals, the Bureau of Mines provides reports, publications, and technical information on a range of topics.

ELIGIBILITY: To lease mineral deposits, you must be (a) a U.S. citizen at least 21 years old; (b) an association of such citizens, including partnerships; or (c) a domestic corporation. The requirements are essentially the same for persons wishing to purchase minerals. Anyone may receive information from the Bureau of Mines.

HOW TO APPLY: Mineral lease applications should be filed on forms specified in Title 43 code of Federal Regulations Part 3000 et seq. The first year's rental must be paid in advance. A $10 filing fee is required.

For instructions on buying minerals, contact the Bureau of Land Management.

For information on minerals, send a letter to:

> Mineral Resources and Environmental Development
> Bureau of Mines
> Department of the Interior
> Washington, D.C. 20240

FOR MORE INFORMATION (on leasing and sales):

> Bureau of Land Management
> Department of the Interior
> Washington, D.C. 20240

RELATED PROGRAMS: Timber Sales and Free Usage

SOIL AND WATER SERVICES

PROGRAM: The Soil Conservation Service of the Department of Agriculture provides technical assistance to individuals and groups in planning and applying soil and water conservation plans. Soil surveys of counties may also be obtained from this agency.

ELIGIBILITY: Owners and operators of private lands, as well as units of state, county and local governments, zoning and planning bodies and similar agencies, are eligible.

HOW TO APPLY: Contact the local Soil Conservation District.

FOR MORE INFORMATION: Soil Conservation Service
Department of Agriculture
Washington, D.C. 20250

RELATED PROGRAMS: Emergency Conservation Measures
Great Plains Conservation
Rural Environmental Assistance
Soil and Water Loans
Water Bank Program

SOIL AND WATER LOANS

PROGRAM: The Farmers Home Administration provides both direct and guaranteed or insured loans to persons needing financing for soil and water conservation programs and related farmland improvements.

ELIGIBILITY: Applicants must (a) be unable to obtain credit from other sources at reasonable terms and conditions; (b) be of legal age; (c) be of good character; and (d) have the necessary experience, training and managerial ability to carry out the proposed operation.

HOW TO APPLY: FHA Form 410-1, "Application for FHA Services," should be filed at the local county office of the Farmers Home Administration.

FOR MORE INFORMATION: Farmers Home Administration
Department of Agriculture
Washington, D.C. 20250

RELATED PROGRAMS: Soil and Water Services

GREAT PLAINS CONSERVATION

PROGRAM: The Soil Conservation Service will share the cost of soil and water conservation measures deemed necessary to protect and stabilize a farm or ranch unit against the climatic and erosional hazards of the Great Plains area.

ELIGIBILITY: The applicant must have control of the land for the period of the contract, which runs from three to ten years.

HOW TO APPLY: An application on Form GP-1 (Rev.), "Application for Participation in Great Plains Conservation Program," should be made to the nearest Soil Conservation Service district conservationist.

FOR MORE INFORMATION: Soil Conservation Service
Department of Agriculture
Washington, D.C. 20250

RELATED PROGRAMS: Rural Environmental Assistance
Soil and Water Conservation
Water Bank Program

RURAL ENVIRONMENTAL ASSISTANCE (REAP)

PROGRAM: The Agricultural Stabilization and Conservation Service encourages farmers, ranchers and woodland owners to carry out plans for conservation (soil, water, woodland and wildlife) and pollution abatement (water, air and land). Assistance is usually in the form of cost-sharing, generally divided equally between REAP and the agricultural participant.

ELIGIBILITY: Any person who as owner, landlord, tenant or sharecropper on a farm or ranch bears a part of the cost of an approved pollution abatement or conservation practice is eligible to apply for cost-share assistance.

HOW TO APPLY: Apply on Form ACP-245 at the Agricultural Stabilization and Conservation Service county office for the county in which the land is located.

FOR MORE INFORMATION: Agricultural Stabilization and
                          Conservation Service
                          Department of Agriculture
                          Washington, D.C. 20250

RELATED PROGRAMS: Emergency Conservation Measures
                     Soil and Water Loans
                     Soil and Water Services
                     Water Bank Program

WATER BANK PROGRAM

PROGRAM: This new program of the Agricultural Stabilization and Conservation Service (ASCS) provides both grants and advisory services and counseling aimed at preserving important breeding and nesting areas of migratory waterfowl.

In return for annual payments for a period of ten years, participants must agree not to drain, burn, fill or otherwise destroy the wetland character of the areas or to use them for agricultural purposes.

ELIGIBILITY: Landowners and operators of specified types of wetlands in designated important migratory waterfowl nesting and breeding areas.

HOW TO APPLY: Letters are sent to persons eligible to participate. Applications may be made any time prior to the announced closing date at the ASCS County office for the county in which the land is located.

FOR MORE INFORMATION: Conservation and Land Use Programs Division
Agricultural Stabilization and Conservation
   Service
Department of Agriculture
Washington, D.C. 20250

RELATED PROGRAMS: Great Plains Conservation
Rural Environmental Assistance
Soil and Water Conservation
Wildlife Research Information

CHAPTER 7

Civil Rights

Discrimination is always ugly. But Federal laws have now made it not only ugly, but often illegal as well.

As an American citizen, you may not be discriminated against in your rights to vote, to acquire an education, to obtain housing and employment, and to enjoy public facilities and accomodations.

It would be naive to deny that discrimination continues to exist, and that governments at Federal, state, and local levels often emphasize political expediency rather than equality under the law.

Nevertheless, it is important that citizens know what their Federal civil rights are and where to go if these rights have been or are in danger of being violated. Congresses passed and Presidents signed these laws; you should not hesitate to demand their enforcement. Nor should you be leery of seeking assistance from your elected officials if you feel you are not getting a satisfactory response. A little "heat" from a Senator or Representative may go a long way toward ending a discriminatory practice.

PROTECTION OF VOTING RIGHTS

PROGRAM: Citizens have the right to vote in all elections without discrimination because of race, religion, or creed. Citizens also receive protection against literacy tests and requirements concerning age and length of residency for presidential elections.

ELIGIBILITY: All U.S. citizens old enough to vote.

HOW TO APPLY: If you believe you need protection of your right to vote, contact the office listed below.

FOR MORE INFORMATION: Voting and Public Accomodation Section
Civil Rights Division
Department of Justice
Washington, D.C. 20530

RELATED PROGRAMS: Clearinghouse Services and Civil Rights Complaints

DESEGREGATION OF PUBLIC EDUCATION

PROGRAM: Your children have the right to an equal education, regardless of their race, color, religion, or national origin.

The Justice Department may go to court to obtain an order to desegregate a public school or public college. The Attorney General may act on the basis of a meritorious complaint from (a) any parent or group of parents whose minor children are being deprived of equal protection of the laws by a school board; or (b) any individual or parent of an individual who has been denied admission to or not permitted to continue in attendance at a public college because of race, color, religion, or national origin.

The Department of Justice may not bring suit unless the person complaining is unable to sue, either because of financial reasons or intimidation.

ELIGIBILITY: See above.

HOW TO APPLY: Contact the office listed below.

CIVIL RIGHTS

FOR MORE INFORMATION: Education Section
Civil Rights Division
Department of Justice
Washington, D.C. 20530

RELATED PROGRAMS: Civil Rights Compliance Activities
Clearinghouse Services and Civil Rights Complaints
Community Relations Services

FAIR HOUSING

PROGRAM: Title VIII of the Civil Rights Act of 1968 establishes the right to freedom from discrimination on the basis of race, color, religion, or national origin in connection with the sale, rental and financing of housing. A private suit alleging discrimination may be filed in the appropriate Federal or state court. The Attorney General is also authorized to bring civil actions in Federal courts under certain conditions.

Individuals who feel affected by a discriminatory housing practice may also file a complaint with the Department of Housing and Urban Development (HUD) which will conduct investigations into alleged violations and take action to conciliate complaints.

ELIGIBILITY: All persons.

HOW TO APPLY: Complaints may be sent to any HUD regional or area office, any HUD Insuring Office, or to HUD's Washington office. You may also contact the Housing Section, Civil Rights Division, Department of Justice, Washington, D.C. 20530.

FOR MORE INFORMATION: Assistant Secretary for Equal Opportunity
Department of Housing and Urban Development
Washington, D.C. 20410

RELATED PROGRAMS: Clearinghouse Services and Civil Rights Complaints
Community Relations Services

EQUAL ENJOYMENT OF PUBLIC ACCOMMODATIONS

PROGRAM: Title II of the 1964 Civil Rights Act assures all persons the right of equal access to public lodgings, restaurants and places of entertainment. The Justice Department may go to court for an injunction or other order prohibiting discrimination based on race, color, religion or national origin in the operation of places of public accommodation. The Attorney General may also intervene in a private civil action if he certifies that the case is of general importance.

ELIGIBILITY: All persons.

HOW TO APPLY: If you believe you have been discriminated against in the use of public accommodations, you should contact the office listed below.

FOR MORE INFORMATION: Voting and Public Accommodations Section
Civil Rights Division
Department of Justice
Washington, D.C. 20530

RELATED PROGRAMS: Clearinghouse Services and Civil Rights Complaints

EQUAL ENJOYMENT OF PUBLIC FACILITIES

PROGRAM: Any public facility owned, operated, or managed by or on behalf of any state or subdivision thereof must allow equal use by all persons, without regard to race, color, religion, or national origin. The Attorney General may bring suit for an injunction prohibiting discrimination when he receives a meritorious written complaint from a person who is unable to bring suit himself either because of financial reasons or possible intimidation.

ELIGIBILITY: Individuals.

HOW TO APPLY: Contact the office below.

FOR MORE INFORMATION: Office of Institutions and Facilities
Civil Rights Division
Department of Justice
Washington, D.C. 20530

NOTE: *In fiscal year 1971, the Civil Rights Division only brought two suits to court under this provision, and one of those was against a county jail!*

RELATED PROGRAMS: Clearinghouse Services and Civil Rights Complaints

EQUAL EMPLOYMENT OPPORTUNITY

PROGRAMS: Title VII of the 1964 Civil Rights Act forbids discrimination by employers, labor organizations and employment agencies. The Attorney General is authorized to sue to enjoin a pattern or practice of discrimination in employment.

The Employment Standards Administration of the Department of Labor will investigate complaints regarding failures of Federal contractors to provide equal employment opportunities.

ELIGIBILITY: All persons. To file a complaint with the Employment Standards Administration, a person must be employed by a Government contractor or subcontractor or be in Federally-involved construction.

HOW TO APPLY: If you feel you have been discriminated against in regard to employment opportunity, you should contact the Civil Rights Division of the Department of Justice at the address below.

To apply to the Employment Standards Division, you should complete and submit a "Complaint of Discrimination in Employment Under Government Contracts" which is available from the Office of Federal Contract Compliance, Employment Standards Administration, Department of Labor, Washington, D.C. 20210.

FOR MORE INFORMATION: Employment Section
Civil Rights Division
Department of Justice
Washington, D.C. 20530

RELATED PROGRAMS: Age Discrimination in Employment
Civil Rights Compliance Activities
Clearinghouse Services and Civil Rights Complaints
Job Discrimination—Complaint Investigation
Minimum Wage and Hour Standards
Spanish-Speaking Americans Assistance
Veterans Reemployment Rights

JOB DISCRIMINATION—COMPLAINT INVESTIGATION

PROGRAM: The Equal Employment Opportunity Commission (EEOC) investigates and seeks to conciliate complaints of discrimination in employment based on race, color, religion, sex or national origin.

ELIGIBILITY: Any aggrieved party may file a charge. Individuals knowing of discriminatory practices by an employer, union, employment agency, or by an apprenticeship or training program may provide information to the EEOC and request that a charge be filed by an EEOC Commissioner. This procedure may also be used by aggrieved parties who fear possible retaliation.

HOW TO APPLY: A charge form may be obtained from the EEOC Regional Office nearest you or from the address below.

FOR MORE INFORMATION: Equal Employment Opportunity Commission
1800 G Street NW
Washington, D.C. 20506

RELATED PROGRAMS: Age Discrimination in Employment
Community Relations Service
Equal Employment Opportunity
Minimum Wage and Age Hour Standards

AGE DISCRIMINATION IN EMPLOYMENT

PROGRAMS: The Age Discrimination in Employment Act of 1967 prohibits arbitrary age discrimination in hiring and other employment practices.

Under the Act, persons 40 to 65 years old receive protection from age discrimination by employers of 25 people or more who are engaged (a) in any commerce-affecting industry; (b) by employment agencies serving such employers; or (c) by labor organizations with 25 or more members in a commerce-affecting industry. It is also unlawful for employers, employment agencies or labor organizations to use advertisements indicating any preference, limitation, specification or discrimination based on age.

Exceptions are provided where age is a bona fide occupational qualification, the differentiation is based on reasonable factors other than age, or it is necessary to observe the terms of a bona fide seniority system or employee benefit plan.

ELIGIBILITY: Persons who believe that they have been discriminated against because of age or believe that such discrimination is occurring against others. A two-year statute of limitations applies to the recovery of any amounts owed to a person as a result of a violation of this Act.

HOW TO APPLY: Either personally or in writing to the appropriate local office of the Employment Standards Administration of the Department of Labor.

FOR MORE INFORMATION: Employment Standards Administration
Department of Labor
Washington, D.C. 20210

RELATED PROGRAMS: Job Discrimination–Complaint Investigation

MINIMUM WAGE AND HOUR STANDARDS (FEDERAL WAGE-HOUR LAW)

PROGRAM: The Federal Wage-Hour Law provides for a minimum hourly wage rate, overtime pay, and equal pay for men and women performing the same or substantially equal work. Additional standards apply to child labor.

Federal wage and hour standards apply generally to employers engaged in interstate or foreign commerce or in the production of goods for such commerce. Employees of contractors performing on Federal or Federally-financed construction projects, or providing goods and services to Federal agencies, are subject to special standards.

To the extent deemed necessary to prevent curtailment of employment opportunities, certificates authorizing special minimum wage rates are issued for learners, handicapped workers, full-time students, student workers and apprentices.

ELIGIBILITY: Any employee, unless specifically exempt, is entitled to be paid in accordance with applicable monetary standards. A two-year statute of limitations applies to the recovery of back wages, except in the case of willful violations, where a three-year limitation applies.

HOW TO APPLY: Persons having knowledge of illegal wage and employment practices, and persons requesting additional information concerning these standards are encouraged to write, telephone, or visit the nearest Employment Standards Administration office of the Department of Labor. Information should be provided describing the type of business and the nature of the work performed. The names of persons making inquiries are treated in complete confidence.

FOR MORE INFORMATION: Employment Standards Administration
Department of Labor
Washington, D.C. 20210

NOTE: *Be sure you also know your state's minimum wage laws.*

RELATED PROGRAMS: Equal Employment Opportunity

FEDERAL WAGE GARNISHMENT LAW

PROGRAM: The Consumer Credit Protection Act limits the amount of an employee's wages or salary which may be garnished, and prohibits employers from discharging employees because of garnishment arising from any one indebtedness.

The general rules for applying the Federal restrictions on garnishment are: (a) if an individual's weekly disposable earnings are $64 or less, only the amount in excess of $48 may be garnished; (b) if weekly disposable earnings are in excess of $64, no more than 25 per cent of such earnings may be garnished.

These restrictions do not apply to earnings witheld by court order for the support of any person, or under Federal bankruptcy proceedings for wage-earners. They also do not apply to debts due for state or Federal taxes. In addition, garnishments issued under the laws of any state may be exempted from the operation of the Federal law where the Secretary of Labor determines that such laws provide substantially similar restrictions.

ELIGIBILITY: Any person whose earnings have been subjected to garnishment is entitled to the protection of these provisions.

HOW TO APPLY: Persons seeking additional advice or assistance concerning the application of the Federal Wage Garnishment Law to specific situations, including persons seeking remedies to illegal actions under the law, should contact the nearest office of the Employment Standards Administration of the Department of Labor. Unless otherwise authorized, the names of persons making inquiries are held in strict confidence.

FOR MORE INFORMATION: Administrator
Employment Standards Administration
Department of Labor
Washington, D.C. 20210

RELATED PROGRAMS: Consumer Affairs

CIVIL RIGHTS COMPLIANCE ACTIVITIES

PROGRAM: The Department of Health, Education and Welfare is responsible for assuring that beneficiaries of more than 250 major programs receive services without discrimination or segregation. This aid is provided through state agencies, school districts, nursing homes, hospitals, colleges, child-care institutions and social service agencies.

ELIGIBILITY: Anyone who believes that he or she has been discriminated against in the provision of the above services in regard to race, color or national origin may file a complaint or grievance with the Office for Civil Rights. The Office will investigate and take corrective steps to assure equal opportunity.

HOW TO APPLY: Send a formal complaint to the Office for Civil Rights.

FOR MORE INFORMATION: Office for Civil Rights
Office of the Secretary
Department of Health, Education and Welfare
Washington, D.C. 20202

RELATED PROGRAMS: Clearinghouse Services and Civil Rights Complaints

CLEARINGHOUSE SERVICES AND CIVIL RIGHTS COMPLAINTS

PROGRAM: The Commission on Civil Rights provides civil rights information to the public, with emphasis on how Federal programs and policy can be used to achieve equal opportunities for minority citizens and to achieve desegregation and integration.

The Commission also receives, investigates and refers complaints alleging denial of civil rights because of race, color, religion or national origin.

ELIGIBILITY: Anyone can seek information or file a complaint.

HOW TO APPLY: Direct request to the Commission.

FOR MORE INFORMATION: United States Commission on Civil Rights
Washington, D.C. 20425

RELATED PROGRAMS: Civil Rights Compliance Activities
Spanish-Speaking Americans Assistance
Veterans Information and Assistance

INDIAN SERVICES

PROGRAM: The Bureau of Indian Affairs, Department of the Interior, administers a wide variety of programs for Indians and Indian tribes for the purpose of making available to them the same rights and opportunities open to other Americans. Programs include provisions for education (through college), social services, loans, home improvement, and employment assistance, among others. The Department of Health, Education and Welfare now administers the Indian Health Service program.

ELIGIBILITY: In general, a person must be a member of an Indian tribe served by the Bureau of Indian Affairs. In some cases, a specified amount of Indian blood may be a condition for eligibility.

HOW TO APPLY: Applications and information may be obtained from the nearest field agency or Area Office of the Bureau of Indian Affairs. There is no formal application procedure for health services, which are provided directly through Federal facilities or under contract with community facilities and private physicians and dentists.

RELATED PROGRAMS: Indian Information and Counseling

INDIAN INFORMATION AND COUNSELING

PROGRAM: The National Council on Indian Opportunity provides advice to tribes, organizations and individuals on Indian programs and in some cases becomes an advocate before departments in situations of interest to Indians. The Council also publishes a monthly newsletter describing issues and events of interest to Indians.

ELIGIBILITY: Indians under the supervision of the Federal Government receive first priority; other Indians are next in priority.

HOW TO APPLY: Phone or write the Council to request advice and assistance.

FOR MORE INFORMATION: Director
National Council on Indian Opportunity
Office of the Vice President
Washington, D.C. 20506

RELATED PROGRAMS: Indian Services

SPANISH-SPEAKING AMERICANS ASSISTANCE

PROGRAM: The Cabinet Committee on Opportunities for Spanish-Speaking People provides advisory services and technical assistance for the purpose of insuring that Federal programs reach all Mexican Americans, Puerto Rican Americans, Cuban Americans, and all other Spanish-speaking and Spanish-surnamed Americans. One of the major concerns of the Committee is insuring equal employment opportunities for Spanish-speaking persons within the Federal Government.

ELIGIBILITY: Mexican Americans, Puerto Ricans, Cuban Americans, Spanish Americans and all other U.S. citizens of Hispanic origin, as well as naturalized citizens of Central America, South America or any Hispanic nation who live in the 50 states.

HOW TO APPLY: By letter to the Cabinet Committee on Opportunities for Spanish-Speaking People, fully stating the information or technical assistance needed.

FOR MORE INFORMATION: Cabinet Committee on Opportunities for
Spanish-Speaking People
1707 H Street NW
Washington, D.C. 20506

RELATED PROGRAMS: Citizenship Education
Clearinghouse Services and Civil Rights Complaints
Equal Employment Opportunity

MINORITY BUSINESS ENTERPRISE

PROGRAM: The Office of Minority Business Enterprise (OMBE) in the Department of Commerce seeks to promote the full participation, through business ownership, of socially and economically disadvantaged individuals in a free enterprise system.

Among its several functions, OMBE serves as a national clearinghouse for information on minority business enterprises and provides local-level assistance to minority businessmen and women.

ELIGIBILITY: Any business enterprise, existing or potential, owned or controlled by one or more socially or economically disadvantaged persons, is eligible for assistance.

HOW TO APPLY: Contact any OMBE or Department of Commerce field office or OMBE headquarters in Washington, D.C.

FOR MORE INFORMATION: Division of Field Operations
Office of Minority Business Enterprise
Department of Commerce
Washington, D.C. 20230

RELATED PROGRAMS: Business Services and Information
Minority Business Development
Small Business Services

MINORITY BUSINESS DEVELOPMENT

PROGRAM: The Small Business Administration has the authority to subcontract the performance of Federal procurement contracts to minority enterprises.

ELIGIBILITY: Actual and potential small businessmen and women and, in some cases, members of community groups are eligible.

A small business is one independently owned and operated, but not dominant in its field. The SBA has established other specific criteria for defining small businesses.

HOW TO APPLY: Personal or written application to SBA field offices.

FOR MORE INFORMATION: Office of Minority Industry Relations
1441 L Street
Room 318
Washington, D.C. 20416

RELATED PROGRAMS: Minority Business Enterprises
Small Business Services

CHAPTER 8

Veterans

Question: How do you become eligible for the greatest number of Government benefits?

Answer: Receive an honorable discharge from the Armed Forces.

It's as simple as that. To express its gratitude to the men and women who have completed their military service, the Federal Government offers a sweeping range of benefits worth many thousands of dollars to the informed individuals who capitalize on them.

A college education, with Uncle Sam picking up most, if not all, of the bills . . .

A low-cost loan to buy a house or start a business . . .

Preference on civil service examinations . . .

These are just some of the benefits you'll learn about in the following chapter. The programs and the funding are there, just waiting for you the veteran (and, in many cases, a widow or other dependents as well) to take advantage of them.

Most of the programs for veterans are managed by the Veterans Administration (VA). If you would like more information on any specific VA program or benefit, you should write or visit the nearest office. *Do not* write the VA Central Office in Washington, D.C.

A valuable and inexpensive reference for persons interested in learning more about veterans benefits is VA Fact Sheet IS-1, "Federal Benefits for Veterans and Dependents." It is available for $.30 from the Superintendent of Documents, U.S. Government Printing Office, Washington, D.C. 20402.

VETERANS EDUCATIONAL ASSISTANCE
(GI BILL)

PROGRAM: As a way of thanking those who serve in the Armed Forces, the GI Bill provides significant financial assistance to persons who either might not otherwise be able to meet the expenses of higher education or who had their education interrupted by active duty after January 31, 1955.

The veteran may select a program to attain an educational, professional or vocational objective at any approved educational institution. Enrollment in courses deemed avocational or recreational in nature will not be approved. A veteran who must complete high school training to qualify for higher education may receive necessary educational assistance without reducing the basic entitlement under this program.

For full-time attendance at an institution, the GI Bill provides, *per month,* $175 to the veteran with no dependents; $205 with one dependent; $230 with two dependents; and $13 for each additional dependent. Part-time students receive a proportional allotment.

ELIGIBILITY: The veteran must have served honorably on active duty for more than 180 days, with at least part of that time occurring after January 31, 1955, or else must have been discharged after that date because of a service-connected disability.

A serviceman who has served on active duty for more than 180 days and who continues on active duty is also eligible. Upon completion of 18 months of active duty, the maximum of 36 months of educational assistance will be provided for at the rate of 1 1/2 months for each month of service.

Certification of enrollment and attendance must be made by both the veteran and the educational institution for each period for which assistance is sought.

Generally, eligibility ends at the date of the veteran's last release from active duty after January 31, 1955. Veterans discharged prior to June 1, 1966 have eight years from that date to complete their schooling.

HOW TO APPLY: An application (VA Form 21 E-1990 for a veteran; VA Form 21 E-1990 for a serviceman) may be obtained from any VA office or regional office and submitted to the regional office.

NOTE: *In fiscal year 1971, 1,584,866 trainees received payments under the GI Bill. This program is undoubtedly one of the most valuable of all Government benefits.*

WAR ORPHANS AND WIDOWS EDUCATIONAL ASSISTANCE

PROGRAM: This program provides partial educational support to qualified members of the families of deceased or disabled veterans, prisoners of war, or servicemen listed as missing in action.

Assistance is in the form of monthly payments for a period of up to 36 months. For full time attendance at an institution, monthly payments are $175; three quarters time, $128; half time, $81.

ELIGIBILITY: Wives, widows, and sons and daughters of (a) veterans who died from service-connected disabilities; (b) living veterans whose service-connected disabilities are considered permanent and total; (c) those who died from any cause while such disabilities were in existence; (d) servicemen who have been listed for a total of 90 days as missing in action; and (e) prisoners of war.

The period of eligibility for a wife or widow extends to November 30, 1976; or for eight years from the date the veteran was first found to have a service-connected total and permanent disability, or from his date of death, whichever is later; of 90 days from the date the serviceman was listed as missing in action or a prisoner of war.

HOW TO APPLY: VA Form 21 E-5490 may be obtained from any VA office or regional office and submitted to the appropriate regional office.

RELATED PROGRAMS: Compensation and Pension for Disabled Veterans
Death Compensation and Pension
Educational Opportunity Grants
Guaranteed Student Loan Program
National Defense Student Loans
Veterans Educational Assistance (GI Bill)

VETERANS REEMPLOYMENT RIGHTS

PROGRAM: If you serve on active or training duty in the Armed Forces or leave your job to be examined for military duty, you have certain rights in relation to getting your job (and benefits) back. This program will assist you in taking advantage of these reemployment rights.

ELIGIBILITY: Persons (including reservists and National Guardsmen) who have served on active duty, active duty for training or training duty with the Armed Forces; or persons who have applied for enlistment or have been called for induction into the Armed Services (including Reserve components) but were found not qualified.

There is no deadline for application to the Department of Labor for assistance in this regard. Deadlines do exist, however, for application to employers in order to qualify for reemployment rights.

HOW TO APPLY: Contact the nearest Department of Labor, Labor Management Services Administration regional or area office.

FOR MORE INFORMATION: Office of Veterans Reemployment Rights
Department of Labor
Washington, D.C. 20210

RELATED PROGRAMS: Federal Employment Preference for Veterans
Veterans Information and Assistance

FEDERAL EMPLOYMENT PREFERENCE
FOR VETERANS

PROGRAM: Wartime veterans and certain dependents wanting to work for the Federal Government receive special preference on Civil Service examinations. Honorably discharged veterans have five points added to their earned eligibility ratings, while disabled veterans and certain wives, widows, and mothers of veterans receive 10 extra points. Vietnam veterans may be eligible for noncompetitive appointments in grades 1 through 5 of the Civil Service.

ELIGIBILITY: All honorably discharged veterans who served in the Armed Forces during a period of war are eligible for civil service preference.

Veterans with no more than 14 years of education who served on or after August 5, 1964 are eligible for the noncompetitive appointments for one year after separation or one year after release from hospitalization or treatment following separation. Employment on the basis of a noncompetitive appointment is contingent on participation in a program of education or training.

All veterans are eligible for advisory services and counseling on Federal employment at Civil Service Commission offices.

HOW TO APPLY: Application forms are available from Job Information Centers at Area Offices of the U.S. Civil Service Commission and from most Post Offices. Veterans eligible for noncompetitive appointments may also personally contact any Federal agency.

NOTE: *A recipient of the Purple Heart qualifies for a 10-point preference.*

FOR MORE INFORMATION: Manpower Sources Division
Bureau of Recruiting and Examining
U.S. Civil Service Commission
Washington, D.C. 20415

RELATED PROGRAMS: Civil Service Employment
Employment Service
Veterans Information and Assistance
Veterans Reemployment Rights
Vocational Rehabilitation for Disabled Veterans

EXEMPLARY REHABILITATION CERTIFICATES

PROGRAM: Ex-servicemen and women who received less than honorable discharges from the Armed Forces but would like to show prospective employers tangible evidence of "having gotten their heads together" after separation may apply to the Secretary of Labor for exemplary rehabilitation certificates. Such a certificate does not in any way change the nature of the original discharge or alter the ex-serviceperson's eligibility for other veterans benefits.

ELIGIBILITY: Any ex-serviceperson who received a less than honorable discharge at least three years earlier and feels that he or she has been self-rehabilitated is eligible to apply.

HOW TO APPLY: Application packets including required forms and instruction sheets are available upon request from the U.S. Department of Labor, Manpower Administration (METTX), Washington, D.C. 20210.

NOTE: *In fiscal year 1971, 1,013 certifications were requested, but only 76 were issued. Not a very high ratio by anyone's standards.*

FOR MORE INFORMATION: Administrative and Management Liaison Staff
Employment Service
Manpower Administration
U.S. Department of Labor
Washington, D.C. 20210

RELATED PROGRAMS: Employment Service

VOCATIONAL REHABILITATION FOR DISABLED VETERANS

PROGRAM: The Veterans Administration will pay the total cost of tuition, books, fees, and training supplies for veterans with service-connected disabilities who qualify for vocational rehabilitation.

During such training and for two months after rehabilitation, a veteran will receive a subsistence allowance in addition to his disability compensation. These monthly allowances range from $118 to $210 plus $6 for each dependent in excess of two unless the veteran receives additional compensation for such dependents. Non-interest bearing loans up to $100 may be advanced to participants in the program.

ELIGIBILITY: Veterans of World War II and later service who, as a result of a service-connected compensable disability, are found to be in need of vocational rehabilitation to overcome their handicap.

Generally, vocational rehabilitation must be accomplished within nine years from the date of discharge from service. Since the normal maximum training time is four years, it is recommended that veterans apply well in advance of the final four years of their nine-year period.

HOW TO APPLY: VA Form 21 E-1900 may be obtained from any VA office or regional office and submitted to the appropriate regional office.

RELATED PROGRAMS: Federal Employment Preference for Veterans
Prosthetics Services

LIFE INSURANCE FOR VETERANS (GI INSURANCE)

PROGRAM: The VA provides life insurance protection for veterans of both World Wars and Korea, and also for service-disabled Vietnam veterans. Mortgage protection life insurance is provided for veterans who have received a VA grant to secure specially adapted housing.

In addition to settlement upon death, life insurance permanent plans provide that the insured may surrender the policy for cash or may be granted a loan up to 94 per cent of the plan's cash surrender value. Dividends are paid only on the life insurance plans for veterans of the two World Wars.

ELIGIBILITY: The only programs open for new issues are the Service-Disabled Insurance and the Mortgage Protection Life Insurance. A veteran discharged from active military duty, who has a service-connected disability for which compensation would be payable if 10 per cent or more in degree, and who is otherwise insurable (in relation to health), who applies for such coverage within one year from the date of notice of the VA service-connected rating, may be issued Service-Disabled Insurance. A veteran who has been given a VA grant for specially adapted housing and who has supplied requested information will be sent notice he is automatically insured for mortgage protection.

HOW TO APPLY: The veteran normally is the only one who may apply for either type of insurance. However, if the veteran is mentally incompetent, a duly appointed guardian may apply in his behalf for Service-Disabled Insurance. Any other person may apply in behalf of the incompetent veteran who is also totally disabled and qualified for waiver of premiums.

Upon receipt of the VA's notice of eligibility for Service-Disabled Insurance, a veteran may submit an application on VA form 29-4364. VA pamphlet 29-9a provides information on selecting a type of policy. (Both the form and the pamphlet may be obtained from the nearest VA office.) Veterans living in states east of the Mississippi River should send the application to: Veterans Administration Center P.O. Box 8079 Philadelphia, Pa. 19101, while Veterans living west of the Mississippi should send to: Veterans Administration Center Federal Building Fort Snelling St. Paul, Minnesota 55111.

RELATED PROGRAMS: Compensation and Pension for Disabled Veterans
Death Compensation and Pension
Housing for Totally Disabled Veterans
Social Security Disability Insurance
Social Security Survivors Insurance

VETERANS BUSINESS AND FARM LOANS

PROGRAMS: These programs provide guarantees or insurance for lenders on loans made to eligible veterans for business or farm purposes.

ELIGIBILITY: World War II and Korean veterans who served 90 days or more active duty and were not dishonorably discharged, or who served less time but were discharged with a service-connected disability, are eligible for both business and farm loans. Veterans who served on active duty for more than 180 days, any part of which was after January 31, 1955, are eligible only for the farm loans.

Unremarried widows of veterans in these classifications who died in service or of service-connected disabilities are also eligible.

Applicants must have a satisfactory credit record and sufficient present and prospective income to meet loan repayment terms.

HOW TO APPLY: Eligible veterans must locate and apply to a private lender willing to make the loan. The lender must then make application for guaranty or insurance to the VA regional office having local jurisdiction.

NOTE: *A loan for a farm residence owned by a veteran and used as his home is classified as a guaranteed or insured home loan.*

RELATED PROGRAMS: Farm Loans
Small Business Services
Veterans Housing Loans

VETERANS HOUSING LOANS

PROGRAMS: The Veterans Administration provides four kinds of housing loans: (a) Direct Loans and Advances; (b) Direct Loans for Disabled Veterans; (c) Guaranteed and Insured Loans; and (d) Mobile Home Loans.

DIRECT LOANS AND ADVANCES: The VA may make loans up to $21,000 ($25,000 in Alaska) for purchase, construction, repair, alteration or improvement of a veteran's house.

The house must be located in a designated housing credit shortage area and, if the loan is for construction or purchase of a less than year-old residence, must meet VA minimum standards for construction. Furthermore, the veteran must be unable to obtain other financing.

DIRECT LOANS FOR DISABLED VETERANS: Begun in 1971, this program provides loans to assist certain totally disabled veterans in acquiring a suitable housing unit, including special fixtures and facilities made necessary by the veteran's disabilities. The loan limits and restrictions are generally the same as for program (a).

GUARANTEED AND INSURED LOANS: To assist veterans and servicemen in obtaining credit for purchase, construction or improvement of a residence, the VA provides guaranteed and insured home loans.

Guaranteed and insured loans may be used for the same purposes as direct loans and advances and, additionally, for purchasing a housing unit in an approved condominium or refinancing a mortgage on a home owned and occupied by a veteran.

Insurance is available only on loans to World War II and Korean veterans.

MOBILE HOME LOANS: Under a program begun in late 1971, guaranteed or insured loans may be made to assist veterans, servicemen, and certain unremarried widows of veterans in purchasing a new mobile home or a used mobile home that itself is the security for a loan guaranteed or insured by the VA or by another Federal agency.

The maximum loan amount and maturity for mobile homes, which must contain facilities for year-round occupancy, may not exceed (1) $10,000 for 12 years on a loan covering only the purchase of a mobile home; (2) $15,000 for 15 years for the purchase of a mobile home and undeveloped lot (but not to exceed $10,000 for the home); (3) $17,500 for 15 years for the purchase of a mobile home and a developed lot (but not to exceed $10,000 for the home).

ELIGIBILITY: In general, those eligible for housing loans (a), (c) and (d) are (1) veterans of World War II or Korea who served 90 days or more of active duty and received discharge or release under conditions other than dishonorable; (2) veterans who served 181 days or more of active duty, part of which occurred after January 31, 1955, and who received discharge or release under conditions other than dishonorable; (3) any veteran in the above classes with less service but discharged with a service-connected disability; (4) unremarried widows of otherwise eligible veterans who died in service or whose deaths were attributable to service-connected disabilities; and (5) servicemen who have served at least 181 days in active duty status. To receive a mobile home loan, a serviceman must have been on active duty for at least two years.

All applicants for loan programs (a), (c) and (d) must also have a satisfactory credit record and sufficient present and prospective income to meet loan repayment terms. Applicants for mobile home loans must additionally have a maximum home loan guaranty entitlement of $12,500 available for use.

The eligibility requirements for loans program (b), Direct Loans for Disabled Veterans, are identical to those for the program, "Housing for Totally Disabled Veterans."

HOW TO APPLY: For direct loans, apply to the VA office having jurisdiction over the property location. For guaranteed and insured home loans (regular or mobile residences), the veteran must apply to a private lender willing to make the loans. The lender, in turn, applies for guaranty or insurance to the VA regional office having jurisdiction.

RELATED PROGRAMS: Home Mortgage Insurance for Veterans
Housing for Totally Disabled Veterans

MORTGAGE INSURANCE FOR VETERANS

PROGRAM: The Federal Home Administration (FHA) makes insurance available to lenders who provide mortgage loans to veterans. Such loans may be used to finance the purchase of proposed, under construction, or existing one-to-four family housing, as well as to refinance indebtedness on existing housing. Maximum insurable loans for an occupant mortgagor are: 1 family, $33,000; 2 or 3 family, $35,750; 4 family, $41,250.

In most cases, the maximum amount of the loan is 100 per cent of the first $15,000 of estimated value, 90 per cent of the next $10,000, and 85 per cent of the amount over $25,000. The downpayment is the difference between the maximum loan amount and the purchase price of the home, but in no case less than $200. This $200 may be applied to closing costs and prepaid items.

The current maximum interest rate is 7 per cent plus 1/2 per cent for mortgage insurance premiums. The FHA application fee is $40 for existing and $50 for proposed housing. The service charge by the mortgagee may not normally exceed 1 per cent of the total mortgage.

ELIGIBILITY: Any certified veteran is eligible.

HOW TO APPLY: Applications should be submitted to a Housing and Urban Development (HUD) insuring or area office through an FHA-approved mortgagee.

FOR MORE INFORMATION: Assistant Commissioner for Unsubsidized
Insured Housing Programs
Housing Production and Mortgage
Credit/FHA
Department of Housing and Urban
Development
Washington, D.C. 20410

RELATED PROGRAMS: Housing for Totally Disabled Veterans
Mortgage Insurance
Veterans Housing Loans

VETERANS HOSPITALIZATION

PROGRAM: Veterans Administration (VA) hospitals provide a comprehensive range of inpatient medical services to veterans. In the cases of veterans who either need treatment for a service-connected disability or are unable to pay, the VA will also assume transportation costs and incidental expenses.

ELIGIBILITY: The first priority for admission goes to veterans who require treatment for disabilities or diseases incurred or aggravated in military service.

Also eligible, as space permits, are veterans who both (1) have received discharges of other than dishonorable wartime service or have served after January 31, 1955 *and* state under oath that they are unable to pay the cost of necessary care. Veterans 65 or older or receiving pensions will be admitted in this category, regardless of their ability to pay the cost of hospital care.

HOW TO APPLY: Apply directly to any VA hospital, outpatient clinic, regional office, or through any veterans service organization representative. You may also mail VA Form 10-10, "Application for Medical Benefits," to the nearest VA hospital.

NOTE: *Veterans may also be eligible for admission to State Veterans Homes. The Veterans Administration assists in the funding of the 34 State Soldiers Homes.*

RELATED PROGRAMS: Alcohol and Drug Dependence Service
Blind Veterans Rehabilitation Centers
Veterans Outpatient Care

VETERANS OUTPATIENT CARE

PROGRAM: Eligible veterans can receive medical and dental services, medicines and medical supplies on an outpatient basis. The outpatient services are available in VA facilities or, when properly authorized, from approved private physicians in your home town.

ELIGIBILITY: Veterans who have a disability incurred or aggravated in service, veterans entitled to vocational rehabilitation, and military retirees are eligible for outpatient medical services.

Outpatient dental care is available for one year after discharge and will be provided for service-connected non-compensable conditions or disabilities shown to have existed at the time of discharge.

Prescription drugs are available to veterans receiving increased compensation or pension based on need of regular aid and attendance, or to those who are permanently homebound.

HOW TO APPLY: File VA Form 10-7131 to determine your eligibility and then file VA Form 10-2827, "Application for Outpatient Treatment." Forms may be obtained at any VA hospital or outpatient clinic.

Veterans eligible for medicine will receive VA Form 10-1151, "Application to Receive Drugs and Medicine," from the VA. Signed forms constitute application.

RELATED PROGRAMS: Vocational Rehabilitation

PROSTHETICS SERVICES

PROGRAM: The Veterans Administration provides prosthetic appliances and services to disabled veterans to assist them in living and working as productive citizens. Items supplied include artificial limbs and eyes, wheelchairs, aids for the blind, hearing aids, braces, orthopedic shoes, eyeglasses, crutches and canes. The program includes training, repairs, and replacements, when needed.

ELIGIBILITY: Disabled veterans receiving or eligible for VA medical treatment and veterans receiving special monthly compensation or increased pension based on need for regular aid and attendance.

HOW TO APPLY: Eligible veterans, or their authorized representatives, may request prosthetics services by reporting in person to any VA facility, by correspondence, or by telephone.

RELATED PROGRAMS: Automobiles for Disabled Veterans

DOMICILIARY CARE

PROGRAM: To assist disabled veterans in either returning to the community, or, when this is not possible, reaching optimal usefulness in a protective environment, the VA provides domiciliary care in a sheltered setting. For the veterans who have the potential for returning to the community, the care is for a period of one year.

ELIGIBILITY: Veterans discharged from active service for a disability incurred or aggravated in the line of duty or those receiving disability compensation when suffering from permanent disability. Veterans of any war who are unable to defray the cost of necessary domiciliary care are also eligible.

HOW TO APPLY: Fill out VA Form 10-10 at any VA office.

RELATED PROGRAMS: U.S. Soldiers Home

U.S. SOLDIERS HOME

PROGRAM: The Defense Department provides a permanent residence for the relief and support of elderly, invalid or disabled soldiers and airmen.

ELIGIBILITY: Former warrant officers and enlisted personnel of the Regular Army and Air Force with one of the following qualifications: (a) honest and faithful service for 20 years or more; (b) a service-connected disability rendering them unable to earn a livelihood; (c) a nonservice-connected disability rendering them unable to earn a livelihood, providing they served during a war.

HOW TO APPLY: Apply by letter to the address below.

FOR MORE INFORMATION: Secretary
Board of Commissioners
U.S. Soldiers Home
Washington, D.C. 20315

RELATED PROGRAMS: Domiciliary Care

ALCOHOL AND DRUG DEPENDENCE SERVICE

PROGRAM: Provides medical, social and vocational rehabilitation to alcohol and drug dependent veterans.

ELIGIBLITY: Any veteran who requires treatment for alcohol or drug dependence is eligible if he or she has been discharged with other than dishonorable wartime service, or has served after January 31, 1955 and states under oath an inability to pay the cost of necessary care. In addition, any veteran who receives a pension or is 65 years of age or older, regardless of ability to pay, is eligible.

HOW TO APPLY: Apply directly to any VA hospital, outpatient clinic, regional office, or through any veterans service organization representative or by mailing VA Form 10-P-10 (Application for Hospital Treatment) to the nearest VA hospital.

RELATED PROGRAMS: Narcotic Addict Treatment
Veterans Hospitalization

BLIND VETERANS REHABILITATION CENTERS

PROGRAM: Blind rehabilitation centers have been established at selected VA hospitals to provide personal and social adjustment programs in addition to any necessary medical or health-related services for blind veterans.

ELIGIBILITY: Any blind veteran who meets the eligibility requirements for admission to a VA hospital.

HOW TO APPLY: Application may be made through any VA hospital or out-patient clinic by completing VA Form 10-10.

RELATED PROGRAMS: Veterans Hospitalization

AUTOMOBILES FOR DISABLED VETERANS

PROGRAM: This program provides financial assistance to disabled veterans for the purchase price of an automobile or other conveyance, as well as additional adaptive equipment necessary for operation. Adaptive equipment may be repaired, replaced, or reinstalled, but only one conveyance may be purchased with assistance at any one time.

ELIGIBILITY: Veterans of World War II or Korea, with honorable service, who have a service-connected disability due to loss or permanent loss of use of one or both feet, one or both hands, or a permanent impairment of vision of both eyes to a prescribed degree. Veterans who incurred the above disabilities on or after February 1, 1955 are eligible if the disabilities were incurred in the line of duty as a direct result of military performance. Servicemen and women on active duty are eligible under the same criteria as World War II and Korean veterans.

NOTE: *Presently, the maximum amount of financial assistance toward the purchase price of a vehicle is $2,800.*

RELATED PROGRAMS: Prosthetics Services

HOUSING FOR TOTALLY DISABLED VETERANS

PROGRAM: The Veterans Administration assists totally disabled veterans in acquiring suitable housing units including special fixtures and facilities necessitated by the nature of the disabilities. The program provides 50 per cent of the cost to the veteran to construct, remodel or pay off a mortgage on a suitable home.

ELIGIBILITY: Veterans with permanent, total and compensatable disabilities due to (a) loss or loss of use of both lower extremities to the extent that mechanical assistance is necessary for movement; or (b) blindness in both eyes (or only perception of light), plus loss or loss of use of one lower extremity; or (c) loss or loss of use of one lower extremity with side effects precluding movement.

HOW TO APPLY: Determination of basic eligibility may be made on VA Forms 10-4555-b and 26-4555 (available at any VA office) to the VA regional office maintaining the veteran's claim folder.

NOTE: *Presently, the amount of the grant may not exceed $12,500.*

RELATED PROGRAMS: Home Mortgage Insurance for Veterans
Life Insurance for Veterans (GI Insurance)
Veterans Housing Loans

COMPENSATION AND PENSIONS FOR DISABLED VETERANS

PROGRAMS: The VA provides compensation to veterans with service-connected disabilities and monthly pensions to veterans in need whose nonservice-connected disabilities prevent them from following a substantially gainful occupation.

The compensation to veterans with service-connected disabilities is computed on the average reduction in earning capacity such disability would cause in civilian occupation. Basic rates of compensation presently range from $25 a month for a 10 per cent degree of disability under wartime conditions to a maximum of $1,120 a month for specified disabilities involving anatomical loss or the loss of use of arms, legs, or for blindness.

Monthly pension rates for veterans with nonservice-connected disabilities, on the other hand, range from $22 for a single veteran to $150 for a veteran with three dependents. Additional allowances of $44 and $100 a month, respectively, are paid if a veteran is housebound or requires aid and attendance.

ELIGIBILITY: Veterans who have suffered disabilities due to service in the Armed Forces are eligible for compensation (the disabilities must be shown to have been incurred in or aggravated by service in the line of duty).

To qualify for a pension, you must have had 90 or more days of active wartime service (or, if less than 90 days, must have been released or discharged because of a service-connected disability) and be permanently and totally disabled. Veterans 65 years of age and older considered permanently and totally disabled are also eligible. To receive a pension, a veteran may not have an annual income in excess of $3,800 if married or with a child, and $2,600 if single.

HOW TO APPLY: Application forms for compensation and pension may oe obtained from a VA office or regional office and submitted to the regional office.

RELATED PROGRAMS: Life Insurance for Veterans
War Orphans and Widows Educational Assistance

DEATH COMPENSATION AND PENSION

PROGRAMS: The Veterans Administration provides compensation to survivors of veterans who died because of a service-connected disability. It also provides a pension as a partial means of support for needy survivors of deceased *wartime* veterans whose deaths were not due to service.

ELIGIBILITY: Persons eligible for death compensation are surviving unremarried widows, children and parents of veterans who died because of a service-connected disability. The compensation is significantly higher for survivors of veterans who died on or after January 1, 1957. No amount is payable to a surviving parent if his income is more than $2,600 annually, or if living with his spouse or remarried, their combined annual income is more than $3,800.

Unmarried widows and children of deceased veterans may be eligible for pensions if the deceased had at least 90 days of honorable *active wartime* service or, if less than 90 days, was discharged for a service-connected disability. An unremarried widow without a child cannot have an income of more than $2,600 annually (or $3,800 with a child). Such child generally must be unmarried and no older than 18 (or under 23 if in school). Pensions are not payable to persons with large estates.

HOW TO APPLY: Application forms for death compensation and widows' pensions may be obtained from any VA office or regional office and submitted to the regional office.

RELATED PROGRAMS: Life Insurance for Veterans (GI Insurance)
Veterans Business Loans
Veterans Farm Loans
Veterans Housing Loans
War Orphans and Widows Educational Assistance

NATIONAL CEMETERIES

PROGRAM: Burial in national cemeteries.

ELIGIBILITY: All members or former members of the Armed Forces, including the Reserves, whose last service ended honorably, as well as certain of their dependents, are eligible for burial in national cemeteries. In addition to service personnel and veterans, the spouse and minor children (also unmarried adult children incapable of self-support) of an eligible deceased person have the right to be buried in a national cemetery. Certain commissioned officers of the Coast and Geodetic Survey and the Public Health Service are also eligible.

HOW TO APPLY: The person responsible for the funeral arrangements (next of kin or funeral director) should communicate as soon as possible with the superintendent of the national cemetery in which interment is desired, furnishing the deceased's name, rank, serial number, date and place of entry into and separation from last period of active service, date and place of birth and date of death.

NOTE: *44 of the 84 national cemeteries presently have available grave space other than previously reserved gravesites and space for second interments in existing graves.*

FOR MORE INFORMATION: Cemetery Branch, Memorial Division
Office of the Chief of Support Services
Department of the Army
Washington, D.C. 20315

RELATED PROGRAMS: Burial Allowance for Veterans
Memorial Plots in National Cemeteries
Procurement of Headstones and Markers

MEMORIAL PLOTS IN NATIONAL CEMETERIES

PROGRAM: National cemeteries provide space for erection of a memorial to an active-duty decedent whose body is not recovered.

ELIGIBILITY: A close relative of the deceased (spouse, child, parent, brother or sister) may apply.

HOW TO APPLY: Department of Defense Form 1330 should be completed indicating "Memorial Marker" and national cemetery where plot is desired. The completed form should be sent to the Chief of Support Services, Department of the Army, Attention: Memorial Division, Washington, D.C. 20315.

RELATED PROGRAMS: Burial Allowance for Veterans
National Cemeteries
Procurement of Headstones and Markers

PROCUREMENT OF HEADSTONES AND MARKERS

PROGRAM: This program provides headstones and markers for all unmarked graves in national and post cemeteries and, upon application, for the unmarked graves of eligible veterans interred in private cemeteries. Memorial headstones or markers are also furnished for nonrecovered or unidentified remains, or those buried at sea.

ELIGIBILITY: Any close relative of the deceased (spouse, child, parent, grandparent, brother or sister) who will accept responsibility for receiving and erecting a headstone or marker may apply for one. Approval is subject to the determination that the deceased was a member of the Armed Forces who died in service or whose last discharge was honorable.

HOW TO APPLY: Complete DD Form 1330, "Application for Headstone or Marker" and mail to the Chief of Support Services, Headquarters, Department of the Army, Attention: Memorial Division, Wahsington, D.C. 20315. Application forms are available at the above address.

RELATED PROGRAMS: Burial Allowance for Veterans
Memorial Plots in National Cemeteries
National Cemeteries

BURIAL ALLOWANCE FOR VETERANS

PROGRAM: The Veterans Administration pays not more than $250 of the funeral and burial expenses of a deceased veteran. A burial flag will also be provided.

ELIGIBILITY: The person who bore the veteran's burial expenses or the undertaker, if unpaid, is eligible for reimbursement of the burial expense. The next of kin, friend or associate of the deceased veteran is eligible for the flag.

The burial allowance is only payable in the cases of deceased wartime veterans whose discharges were not dishonorable, and peacetime veterans who were discharged or released because of a disability incurred in the line of duty, died of a service-connected disability, or were receiving or entitled to receive compensation at the time of their deaths. A peacetime veteran is eligible for a burial flag if he served at least one enlistment.

HOW TO APPLY: VA Form 21-530 may be obtained from any VA office or regional office and submitted to the regional office.

RELATED PROGRAMS: Death Compensation and Pension
Memorial Plots in National Cemeteries
National Cemeteries
Procurement of Headstones and Markers

CLAIMS OF PRISONERS OF WAR IN VIETNAM

PROGRAM: The Foreign Claims Settlement Commission of the United States provides compensation to members of the Armed Forces who were held as prisoners of war for any period of time during the Vietnam War. Payment is at the rate of $2 per day for each day that the prisoner failed to receive the quality or quantity of food prescribed by the Geneva Convention, and an additional $3 per day for each day that the hostile force failed to meet the conditions and requirements outlined by that Convention in respect to labor of prisoners or inhuman treatment (total of $5 per day).

ELIGIBLITY: Any regular serviceman held as a prisoner of war by a hostile force during the Vietnam War after February 28, 1961.

In the case of death of any prisoner of war, compensation is payable, in order of preference, to (a) widow or husband; (b) widow or husband and children; (c) child or children, if there is no widow or husband; and (d) parents, if there is no widow, husband, or child.

Excluded from benefits are members of the Armed Forces who, while held by the enemy, at any time voluntarily, knowingly, and without duress gave aid to or collaborated with the hostile force.

Claims must be filed on or before June 24, 1973, or three years after the prisoner of war has returned to the jurisdiction of the United States, or three years after the date the Department of Defense makes a determination that the prisoner of war is deceased or presumed to be dead, whichever date occurs last.

HOW TO APPLY: Formal claim applications are required to be filed directly with the Foreign Claims Settlement Commission of the United States. Upon receipt, claims will be acknowledged, docketed, and claim number assigned.

FOR MORE INFORMATION: Office of the General Counsel
Foreign Claims Settlement Commission of the
  United States
Washington, D.C. 20579

RELATED PROGRAMS: None

VETERANS INFORMATION AND ASSISTANCE

PROGRAM: VA Veterans Assistance Personnel provide information and assistance on all benefits legislated by Congress. They will help the veteran or dependent file claims, secure supporting evidence and, on request, represent the claimant before the VA adjudicative or medical authorities. Special emphasis is placed on the recently separated disabled serviceman.

Service includes providing information and personal service on matters which affect veterans but are under the jurisdiction of other Federal, state, county or local agencies.

For the recently separated serviceman, Veterans Assistance Centers (US-VAC) have been established in 72 cities to provide onestop service and counseling.

In trying to facilitate the readjustment of veterans to civilian life, USVAC's pay special attention to the needs of veterans with less than a high school education. USVAC's also service as a central point to furnish civil rights information to veterans and to receive and initiate action on discrimination complaints.

ELIGIBLITY: Veterans, their dependents or beneficiaries, their representatives or other interested parties are eligible for information and assistance. The Veterans Assistance Centers generally emphasize service to recently discharged or released veterans.

HOW TO APPLY: Phone or visit the nearest VA regional office or Veterans Assistance Center.

RELATED PROGRAMS: Federal Employment Preference for Veterans
Veterans Reemployment Rights

CHAPTER 9

Disaster Relief

"Tornado damage to run into millions."
"Thousands homeless after storm."
"Drought perils crop harvest."
Headlines such as these are, unfortunately, not unusual. For almost every week of the year, some part of the country falls victim to a natural disaster. Sometimes the area affected is relatively small—a few towns or possibly just one. At other times, the damage caused by a major disaster such as tropical storm Agnes in 1972 may extend over several states.

Much as it might like to, the Federal Government has no programs guaranteed to prevent catastrophes. But when a disaster does occur, victims may be able to obtain financial or material assistance from one or more programs designed to assist survivors in rebuilding and re-establishing a normal pattern of living.

The benefits described in this chapter are ones that we hope you never have to seek. But, if a major disaster does strike, it's important to know what the Federal Government can do to help you.

DISASTER ASSISTANCE

PROGRAM: The Office of Emergency Preparedness provides assistance to states, local governments and individuals to alleviate suffering and hardships resulting from major disasters.

Post-disaster services to individuals include removal of wreckage and debris, performance of essential protective work on private lands, provisions for emergency shelter and temporary housing, and assistance to the unemployed.

ELIGIBILITY: Disaster victims in a declared major disaster area.

HOW TO APPLY: Individuals should apply to their state and local governments. Applications normally must be submitted within 90 days of the major disaster declaration.

FOR MORE INFORMATION: Disaster Assistance Division
Disaster Operations Office
Office of Emergency Preparedness
Washington, D.C. 20504

RELATED PROGRAMS: Economic Injury Disaster Loans
Emergency Conservation Measures
Emergency Loans
Mortgage Insurance for Disaster Victims
Physical Disaster Loans

PHYSICAL DISASTER LOANS

PROGRAM: The Small Business Administration (SBA) provides loans, at a maximum interest rate of 6 per cent, to victims of physical disasters. Loans, which are made without regard to ability to secure needed funds from private sources, may be used to repair or replace damaged or destroyed realty, machinery and equipment, or household and other personal property.

These loans are not available to persons engaged in agriculture and may not be used, in whole or part, for agricultural purposes.

ELIGIBILITY: Anyone who suffered physical property loss as a result of a disaster which occurred in an area designated as eligible for assistance by the SBA. Individuals, business concerns, churches, private schools, colleges and universities, and hospitals are eligible to apply for assistance.

Eligibility to file ends at the close of the sixth month following the month in which the SBA designated a disaster loan area.

HOW TO APPLY: Applications should be made on a standard form for either a home or business loan and filed with the nearest regular SBA office or special disaster office.

FOR MORE INFORMATION: Office of Disaster Operations
Small Businesss Administration
1441 L Street NW
Washington, D.C. 20416

RELATED PROGRAMS: Economic Injury Disaster Loans
Emergency Loans
Rural Housing Disaster Loans

ECONOMIC INJURY DISASTER LOANS (EIDL)

PROGRAM: The Small Business Administration provides loans to business concerns suffering economic injury as a result of certain Presidential and Department of Agriculture disaster designations.

Loan funds, at a maximum 6 per cent with up to 30 years to repay, may be used to pay current liabilities which the small concern could have paid if the disaster had not occurred. Working capital for a limited period can be provided until business conditions return to normal. No funds are available for realty or equipment repair or acquisition.

ELIGIBILITY: Any small business concern, as described in SBA rules and regulations, is eligible. Evidence of the extent of economic injury must be furnished.

Eligibility deadlines range from six months on Presidential designations to up to one year on Department of Agriculture designations.

HOW TO APPLY: Applications should be filed with the nearest SBA field office on one copy of a standard form which will be provided.

FOR MORE INFORMATION: Office of Disaster Operations
Small Business Administration
1441 L Street NW
Washington, D.C.20416

RELATED PROGRAMS: Emergency Loans
Physical Disaster Loans

EMERGENCY LOANS

PROGRAM: The Farmers Home Administration provides both direct and guaranteed or insured loans to help farmers and ranchers recover from severe losses caused by natural disasters.

Loans are made for operating and living expenses and for (a) replacement of damaged or destroyed equipment and livestock; and (b) real estate repairs made necessary by natural disasters. Subject to certain exceptions, loans are not made to finance major adjustments and expansion in farming and ranching operations or to refinance secured debts.

ELIGIBILITY: To be eligible, an individual must be (a) an established farmer or rancher who manages his operations; (b) a citizen of the United States; (c) a victim of severe property damages or crop loss caused by a major or natural disaster; (d) a person of good character and the ability to succeed; and (e) must be in need of credit.

HOW TO APPLY: An application form provided by the Famers Home Administration must be presented to the FHA county office servicing the applicant. FHA personnel will assist in the completion of the application.

FOR MORE INFORMATION: Farmers Home Administation
Department of Agriculture
Washington, D.C. 20250

RELATED PROGRAMS: Economic Injury Disaster Loans
Emergency Conservation Measures
Rural Housing Disaster Loans

RURAL HOUSING DISASTER (RHD) LOANS

PROGRAM: The Farmers Home Administration makes loans available to assist farm owners to repair, rehabilitate or replace property damaged or destroyed by a natural or major disaster.

ELIGIBILITY: The requirements are the same as the ones for Low to Moderate Income Housing Loans (see chapter on Housing), except that RHD loans may be made without regard to whether needed credit is available from private sources.

HOW TO APPLY: File an application with the county office of the Farmers Home Administration.

FOR MORE INFORMATION: Farmers Home Administration
Department of Agriculture
Washington, D.C. 20250

RELATED PROGRAMS: Emergency Loans
Low to Moderate Income Housing Loans
Physical Disaster Loans

EMERGENCY LIVESTOCK FEED PROGRAM

PROGRAM: Stocks of feed grains may be made available at reduced prices to livestock owners or donated to needy Indian tribes.

ELIGIBILITY: Livestock owners who (a) do not have sufficient feed; (b) have suffered a serious loss of feed; (c) require feed purchases larger than usual because of emergency; and (d) would suffer undue financial hardship in obtaining sufficient feed through normal channels.

Also eligible are members of designated Indian tribes who are without sufficient means to purchase feed after allowances for necessary living expenses.

The Secretary of Agriculture determines eligibility. Need usually arises as a result of severe drought, flood, hurricane, blizzard or other uncontrollable catastrophe.

HOW TO APPLY: Application should be made on Form DF-6 at the Agricultural Stabilization and Conservation Service county office. Indians should make formal application for assistance to authorized personnel at designated offices.

FOR MORE INFORMATION: Agricultural Stabilization and Conservation
Service
Department of Agriculture
Washington, D.C. 20250

or

Bureau of Indian Affairs
Department of the Interior
Washington, D.C. 20242

RELATED PROGRAMS: None

EMERGENCY CONSERVATION MEASURES (ECM)

PROGRAM: The Agricultural Stabilization and Conservation Service provides cost-sharing grants to farmers for emergency conservation measures to control wind erosion on farmlands, or to rehabilitate farmlands damaged by wind erosion, floods, hurricanes or other natural disasters. The Government generally will pay about 80 per cent of the cost of the conservation practice.

ELIGIBILITY: Any owner, landlord, tenant or sharecropper on a farm or ranch, including associated groups, who bears a part of the cost of an approved conservation practice is eligible to apply for cost-share conservation assistance.

HOW TO APPLY: You may apply, at any time of the year, on form ASCS-245 at the Agricultural Stabilization and Conservation Service office in the county in which the land is located.

FOR MORE INFORMATION: Agricultural Stabilization and Conservation Service
Department of Agriculture
Washington, D.C. 20250

RELATED PROGRAMS: Emergency Loans
Rural Environmental Assistance

MORTGAGE INSURANCE FOR DISASTER VICTIMS

PROGRAM: The Federal Housing Administration provides guaranteed or insured loans on mortgages to help victims of a major disaster undertake home ownership.

FHA insures lenders against loss on mortgage loans which may be used to finance the purchase of proposed, under construction or existing single family housing for the occupant mortgagor who is a victim of a major disaster. The maximum insurable loan for such an occupant mortgagor is $14,400.

The current maximum interest rate is 7 per cent plus 1/2 per cent for the mortgage insurance premium. No downpayment is required. The FHA application fee is $40 for existing, and $50 for proposed housing. The service charge varies, but may not normally exceed 1 per cent of the total mortgage.

HOW TO APPLY: The application should be submitted to a Housing and Urban Development insuring or area office through an FHA-approved mortgagee.

FOR MORE INFORMATION: Assistant Commissioner for Unsubsidized
Insured Housing Program
Housing Production and Mortgage
Credit/FHA
Department of Housing and Urban
Development
Washington, D.C. 20410

RELATED PROGRAMS: Mortgage Insurance
Mortgage Insurance for Veterans
Physical Disaster Loans

CIVIL DEFENSE SHELTER INFORMATION

PROGRAM: The Office of Civil Defense (OCD) provides general technical information on civil defense shelters.

ELIGIBILITY: Architects, engineers, home builders, homeowners, and other interested groups.

HOW TO APPLY: Write to state or local civil defense offices, OCD regional offices or headquarters.

FOR MORE INFORMATION: Architectural and Engineering Development
Division
Office of Civil Defense
Washington, D.C. 20310

RELATED PROGRAMS: Civil Defense Medical Self-Help

CIVIL DEFENSE MEDICAL SELF-HELP

PROGRAM: The aim of this program is to provide information and training that will help prepare people for survival in a time of natural or nuclear disaster when the services of health personnel may not be available.

ELIGIBILITY: "With the ultimate goal of one member of each family trained in medical self-help, the main eligibility requirement is interest."

HOW TO APPLY: Letter requests for materials and assistance should be sent to the state medical self-help representative.

FOR MORE INFORMATION: Division of Emergency Health Services
Health Services and Mental Health
Administration
14A-55, Parklawn Building
5600 Fishers Lane
Rockville, Maryland 20852

RELATED PROGRAMS: Civil Defense Shelter Information

CHAPTER 10

Consumer Protection

Do you feel that some company played it fast and loose with you in the stock market?

Are you angry about the quality of phone service?

Would you like to have up-to-date information on how to use and take care of many of the products you have in your house?

You have rights as a consumer, and the Federal Government has been expanding the number of programs designed to protect your interests. Enforcement powers vary according to the particular program, but you at least can have the satisfaction of knowing that your complaints will receive attention.

So if you have a gripe, don't take it straight to the bartender.

Take it to Uncle Sam.

CONSUMER AFFAIRS

PROGRAM: The Office of Consumer Affairs provides information on consumer education, proposed legislation affecting consumers, Federal consumer programs, and private organizations which seek to advance the cause of the consumer. Assistance in resolving consumer complaints is provided when appropriate.

ELIGIBILITY: Individual consumers, business and civic groups, labor unions, trade associations, and state and local governments are all eligible for assistance.

HOW TO APPLY: By letter to the Headquarters Office listed below.

FOR MORE INFORMATION: Office of Consumer Affairs
New Executive Office Building
Room 6003
Washington, D.C. 20506

RELATED PROGRAMS: Consumer Product Information
Federal Wage Garnishment Law
Investor Protection

CONSUMER PRODUCT INFORMATION

PROGRAM: The General Services Administration publishes a quarterly index of selected Government publications on how to buy, use, and take care of consumer products. The Consumer Product Information Index is free. Government publications listed in the index either are available free or are offered for sale at the prices indicated.

ELIGIBILITY: Anyone can request information.

HOW TO APPLY: Visit the nearest Federal Information Center or write to: Consumer Product Information, Washington, D.C. 20407.

FOR MORE INFORMATION: Consumer Product Information Coordinating Center
General Services Administration
Washington, D.C. 20405

RELATED PROGRAMS: Agricultural Information
Consumer Affairs
Federal Information Center
Government Publications
Technical Information

INVESTOR PROTECTION

PROGRAM: Investors who believe they have been defrauded in their securities transactions should contact the Securities and Exchange Commission (SEC), which will investigate all complaints. The public should be aware, however, that the Commission is not a collection agency, nor is it authorized to advise investors whether particular transactions violated the securities laws.

ELIGIBILITY: Anyone may file a complaint or seek information from the Securities and Exchange Commission.

HOW TO APPLY: Contact any SEC office.

FOR MORE INFORMATION: Division of Enforcement
Securities and Exchange Commission
500 North Capitol Street
Washington, D.C. 20549

RELATED PROGRAMS: Consumer Affairs

FEDERAL TRADE COMMISSION

PROGRAM: The Federal Trade Commission investigates acts and practices which may be unfair or deceptive to the consuming public. It also seeks to prevent and eliminate monopolistic practices and unfair methods of competition.

The FTC emphasizes investigation of false and misleading advertising. The Comisssion also protects consumer interests in the areas of credit and reporting, flammable fabrics, fair packaging and labeling, and representations made by salespersons and others in the sale of goods and services in interstate commerce.

Monopolistic practices that the Federal Trade Commission investigates include price-fixing conspiracies, boycotts, price discriminations, and illegal mergers and acquisitions.

ELIGIBILITY: FTC services are available to anyone, free of charge.

HOW TO APPLY: By letter to the Commission, including facsimiles of questioned advertising or labeling, or a summary of any claimed oral misrepresentation, together with the name and address of the alleged offender. Questioned practices used within a single state may be referred to state or local authorities.

FOR MORE INFORMATION: Federal Trade Commission
16th and Pennsylvania Avenue NW
Washington, D.C. 20580

NOTE: *In recent years, the Federal Trade Commission has been one of the staunchest advocates of meaningful consumer protection.*

RELATED PROGRAMS: Consumer Affairs
Consumer Product Information
Livestock and Poultry Market Supervision

INVESTIGATION OF COMMUNICATIONS COMPLAINTS

PROGRAM: Are you upset by the quality of phone service? Do you have a gripe about broadcasting? Why not tell your complaints to the Federal Communications Commission?

The FCC handles and investigates complaints from the public concerning radio and television services and the quality and rates of telephone and telegraph communications. The Commission also provides communications information and education through its Public Information Office in Washington and its field offices.

ELIGIBILITY: Anyone may file a complaint or seek information.

HOW TO APPLY: Most queries and complaints can be handled by FCC field offices. Matters such as equal time for political candidates and fairness in presentation of issues should be directed to the FCC's Complaints and Compliance Division (see address below).

FOR MORE INFORMATION: Complaints and Compliance Division
Broadcast Bureau
Federal Communications Commission
Washington, D.C. 20554

RELATED PROGRAMS: None

COMMODITY EXCHANGE ACT

PROGRAM: The Commodity Exchange Authority investigates complaints of cheating, fraud and manipulative practices in the commodity futures market. The Authority stresses, however, that it is not a collection agency, nor is it authorized either to advise traders whether particular transactions were violations of the Commodity Exchange Act, or to seek recovery in their behalf, through court action or otherwise. The law, however, does provide for penalties against those who have been found guilty, after receiving a proper hearing, of violating the Act.

The Commodity Exchange Authority also provides information on futures trading to the general public.

ELIGIBILITY: Anyone who wishes to engage in or is involved in commodity futures trading may file a complaint or receive information.

HOW TO APPLY: Contact any office of the Exchange Authority orally or in writing.

FOR MORE INFORMATION: Commodity Exchange Authority
Department of Agriculture
Washington, D.C. 20250

RELATED PROGRAMS: Consumer Affairs
Federal Trade Commission
Livestock and Poultry Market Supervision

LIVESTOCK AND POULTRY MARKET SUPERVISION

PROGRAM: The Packers and Stockyards Administration investigates complaints by consumers and producers relating to unfair business practices in the marketing of livestock, meat and poultry. The agency also accepts complaints from members of these industries regarding unfair, deceptive, discriminatory, or monopolistic practices of competitors.

ELIGIBILITY: Anyone may file a complaint.

HOW TO APPLY: Complaints may be submitted orally or in writing to the Washington, D.C. headquarters, or to field offices.

FOR MORE INFORMATION: Packers and Stockyards Administration
Room 3039 South Building
Department of Agriculture
Washington, D.C. 20250

RELATED PROGRAMS: Commodity Exchange Act
Consumer Affairs
Federal Trade Commission

CONSUMER PROTECTION

INTERSTATE COMMERCE COMPLAINTS

PROGRAM: The Interstate Commerce Commission will investigate complaints or inquiries which relate to deficiencies in carrier service, discrimination, or other types of violations by carriers subject to Commission jurisdiction.

ELIGIBILITY: Any person may make an inquiry, request, or complaint.

HOW TO APPLY: By letter, telephone or personal contact with the nearest Interstate Commerce Commission office.

FOR MORE INFORMATION: Interstate Commerce Commission
Washington, D.C. 20423

RELATED PROGRAMS: Investigation of Shipping Complaints

INVESTIGATION OF SHIPPING COMPLAINTS

PROGRAM: The Federal Maritime Commission seeks to settle disputes between carriers and shippers regarding excessive rates or discriminatory practices. Complaints may be settled on an informal basis or, if warranted, by institution of formal proceedings.

ELIGIBILITY: Any person may file a complaint.

HOW TO APPLY: By letter to the Headquarters Office listed below.

FOR MORE INFORMATION: Bureau of Enforcement
Federal Maritime Commission
1405 I Street NW
Washington, D.C. 20573

RELATED PROGRAMS: Interstate Commerce Complaints
Ships—Sales and Mortgage Insurance

CHAPTER 11

Information

If you need information, there's a good chance that some Federal agency can either supply exactly what you're looking for or else give you some good leads.

The trick, then, is knowing where and how to make inquiries within the Federal bureaucracy. There's nothing more frustrating than being shunted from place to place in a seemingly never-ending circle.

The purpose of this chapter is to help you avoid that kind of irritation. We'll show you how to order Government publications covering almost every area of human knowledge, where to go to get some good maps, what services you can obtain from the Library of Congress and the National Archives, and even where to go if you want to find out how old you really are!

The variety of information available from Federal agencies is almost unlimited. It's all there for your benefit (and paid for, need we add, with your tax dollars). So seek, and ye shall find.

Happy hunting!

GOVERNMENT PUBLICATIONS

PROGRAM: You may not have realized it, but Uncle Sam is one of the world's largest publishers. More than 25,000 U.S. Government publications, covering nearly every imaginable field of interest are available for purchase from the Superintendent of Documents or Government Bookstores. (During fiscal 1972 alone, it is estimated that over 5,000,000 sales orders for Government publications were filled.) Many libraries also serve as depositories for Federal publications.

ELIGIBILITY: Anyone may purchase Government publications directly or by mail, or may consult them in depository libraries. In general, there is no restriction on reprinting or quoting from U.S. Government publications.

HOW TO APPLY: There is no application procedure. Mail orders for publications must be accompanied by remittance made payable to the Superintendent of Documents. Interested persons may request that their names be put on the mailing list to receive, without charge, a bi-weekly list of selected United States Government publications. There are also 47 subject price lists which are available without charge.

FOR MORE INFORMATION: Superintendent of Documents
U.S. Government Printing Office
Washington, D.C. 20402

RELATED PROGRAMS: Consumer Product Information
Library of Congress Services
Science Information Exchange
Technical Information

LIBRARY OF CONGRESS SERVICES

PROGRAMS: The Library of Congress provides a large number of technical information programs for interested individuals and organizations. These include publications, general and specialized reference and bibliographic services, photoduplication, and distribution of Library of Congress catalog cards.

Publications include guides to the Library of Congress collections, bibliographies on many subjects, literary brochures and records, a "Quarterly Journal" discussing the Library's collections and programs. The Library of Congress also issues a series of folksong records.

Reference and bibliographic services are available in such diverse fields as American history, science and technology (including specialized services), African, Oriental, Slavic, Central European and Hispanic Studies, children's literature, music, geography, and cartography. Also available are numerous materials including serials, manuscripts, maps, phonorecords, prints, photographs and motion pictures.

In general, guidance is offered in the identification and use of material, and, as time permits, reference service in answer to written requests is extended to correspondents who have exhausted local, state, and regional resources. Persons requiring services which cannot be performed by library staff can be supplied with the names of private researchers who can do the work on a fee basis.

Copies of manuscripts, prints, photographs, maps, and book material are made available upon request. Anyone may request photocopies, but copyrighted or otherwise restricted materials may not be reproduced without special permission. The fees vary according to the nature and complexity of the request.

ELIGIBILITY: Anyone is eligible to apply for Library of Congress services. Admission to the Library itself is free and available to all persons over high school age.

HOW TO APPLY: Walk-in service or written request.

FOR MORE INFORMATION: Library of Congress
Washington, D.C. 20540

RELATED PROGRAMS: Government Publications
National Agricultural Library
Science Information Exchange
Technical Information

NATIONAL ARCHIVES REFERENCE SERVICES

PROGRAM: If you have to do historical research which involves the Federal Government, you probably can find the information in the National Archives or in one of six Presidential libraries or 15 Federal records centers.

Inquiries about records are answered by mail, but information in the records themselves may only be obtained in the research rooms or through the purchase of reproductions.

ELIGIBILITY: Anyone is eligible.

HOW TO APPLY: To see records personally, fill out GSA Form 6769 (Researcher Application). To obtain information or copies by mail, contact the National Archives or depository.

FOR MORE INFORMATION:　Central Reference Division
National Archives and Records Service
General Services Administration
Washington, D.C. 20408

RELATED PROGRAMS:　Library of Congress Services
Smithsonian Institution Programs

NATIONAL AUDIOVISUAL CENTER

PROGRAM: The National Audiovisual Center offers copies of Federal agencies' audiovisual materials to the public. The materials may be purchased, rented, or obtained on loan.

ELIGIBILITY: Anyone is eligible. Materials may not be used for commercial purposes.

HOW TO APPLY: By letter.

FOR MORE INFORMATION: National Audiovisual Center
National Archives and Records Service
General Services Administration
Washington, D.C. 20409

RELATED PROGRAMS: Government Publications
Technical Information

COPYRIGHT SERVICE

PROGRAM: The Copyright Office (a division of the Library of Congress) is responsible for administering the U.S. Copyright Law and as such registers claim to copyright, catalogs all registrations, and provides information to the public about these registrations.

General copyright information is available free of charge. Reports on copyright facts found in the records of the Copyright Office may be obtained for a statutory fee of $5 an hour; however, any member of the public may use the Copyright Card Catalog in the Copyright Office without charge. Fees provided by law for registration of claims to copyright are $6 for all categories except renewals which are $4. There are also separate schedules of statutory fees for recordations of assignments, certified copies of record and similar requests.

ELIGIBILITY: Information will be supplied to anyone who applies. Registration may be made by authors, their assignees, and others designated by law, or by their agents.

FOR MORE INFORMATION: Copyright Office
Library of Congress
Washington, D.C. 20559

RELATED PROGRAMS: Library of Congress Services
Patents and Trademarks

FEDERAL INFORMATION CENTERS

PROGRAM: The Federal Government has been opening Federal Information Centers in major metropolitan areas. The purpose of these Centers is to provide convenient points for the public to address questions about Federal agencies and either receive the desired information immediately or obtain an accurate referral to the office best able to be of assistance.

ELIGIBILITY: Anyone can apply for information.

HOW TO APPLY: Visit, telephone, or write the nearest Federal Information Center.

FOR MORE INFORMATION: Assistant Administrator
General Services Administration
Washington, D.C. 20405

RELATED PROGRAMS: Consumer Product Information
Government Publications
Technical Information

SCIENCE INFORMATION EXCHANGE

PROGRAM: The Smithsonian Institution serves as a clearinghouse for information on current scientific research actually in progress.

Federal agencies and many non-Federal organizations with major research programs cooperate by furnishing the Exchange with information on their current programs and projects. Each research record includes the name of the agency or organization, principal and associate investigators, location of work, level of effort, and dates of work. A 200 word description is also included. All these items are analyzed and indexed to assure retrieval of all records related to a specific research element or topic. Any element or combination of items can be compiled or assembled to answer a variety of questions.

There is a charge made for the cost of retrieving and providing information from the file. Cost and specific products are described in a brochure available from the Exchange.

ELIGIBILITY: All scientific research submitted will be included in the Science Information Exchange. Anyone may reference the file.

HOW TO APPLY: Each principal investigator or the granting organization completes a one-page "notice of research project." To retrieve information from the data on record, the requester should contact the Director of the Exchange, outline his or her requirements, or complete an order form which specifies the needs.

FOR MORE INFORMATION: Smithsonian Science Information Exchange, Inc.
Room 300
Madison National Bank Building
1730 M Street NW
Washington, D.C. 20036

RELATED PROGRAMS: Library of Congress Services
Technical Information

AGE SEARCH

PROGRAM: Would you like to prove that you're older (or younger) than you look? For a modest fee, the Bureau of the Census will conduct a personal age search for you, based on census records. These records may be the only resource if your birth was not registered and if generally acceptable proofs, such as affidavits from the doctor or midwife, family Bible records, or baptismal certificates, are not available.

You may need proof of age in one or more of the following instances: (1) to qualify for Government programs (Medicare, Social Security, etc.); (2) as proof of citizenship (for instance, when obtaining a passport); (3) for employment purposes; (4) to qualify for rights of inheritance; and (5) to obtain annuities and similar rights or benefits to which you may be entitled.

ELIGIBILITY: Personal information from census records of 1900 and later is confidential and may be furnished only upon written request of the person to whom it relates or, for a proper purpose, to a legal representative of an estate. Information regarding a child who has not reached legal age may be obtained upon the written request of either parent.

For records of a deceased person, the application must be signed by one of the following: (1) a blood relative in the immediate family; (2) the surviving wife or husband; (3) a beneficiary; or (4) the administrator or executor of the estate. In all cases, a certified copy of the death certificate as well as a certified copy of the court order naming the legal representative or legal evidence of the beneficiary's relationship to the deceased must be furnished.

HOW TO APPLY: Application form BC-600 can be obtained by request. A $5 fee is charged for the cost of the search and the certification of the results (the fee is $6 for an expedited search). The fee is required whether or not the search is successful.

FOR MORE INFORMATION: Personal Census Service Branch
Social and Economic Statistics Administration
Department of Commerce
Pittsburg, Kansas 66762

RELATED PROGRAMS: None

CENSUS MAPS

PROGRAM: If you need a map, one good place to look is the Bureau of the Census. In addition to the base maps used for censuses and surveys, the Bureau prepares, for inclusion in its published reports, maps of states, cities, counties, minor civil divisions or census county divisions within counties, urbanized areas of standard metropolitan statistical areas, census tracts and congressional districts.

Other maps, prepared for separate publication, include a thematic U.S. map series, a series of county subdivision maps, the "Congressional District Atlas," and metropolitan, county, and place maps for the 1970 census.

ELIGIBILITY: Anyone is eligible to buy Census Bureau maps.

HOW TO APPLY: By written request.

FOR MORE INFORMATION: Data User Services Office
Bureau of the Census
Washington, D.C. 20233

RELATED PROGRAMS: Census Bureau Publications
Map Information

MAP INFORMATION

PROGRAM: The Geological Survey collects and furnishes to potential users information concerning aerial photography, topographic mapping, geodetic and other survey data available for general use from Federal agencies, as well as the sources from which this data may be obtained. Advance copies of Geological Survey maps, aerial photography, and geodetic control notes are provided on a cost basis. There are no restrictions on the use of this information.

ELIGIBILITY: General public.

HOW TO APPLY: Contact the Map Information Office at the address below.

FOR MORE INFORMATION: Map Information Office
Geological Survey
Department of the Interior
Washington, D.C. 20242

RELATED PROGRAMS: Census Maps

CENSUS BUREAU PUBLICATIONS

PROGRAM: The Bureau of the Census provides statistical results, in the form of printed reports and computer tapes, of all censuses authorized by Federal law, as well as periodic and special surveys.

Censuses are made of population, housing, agriculture, irrigation and drainage, business (retail trade, wholesale trade and selected services), construction, transportation, manufacturing, mineral industries, commercial fisheries and governments.

Census laws guarantee the confidentiality of data concerning individual persons, households, farms, and business establishments. Reports contain statistical summaries only.

ELIGIBILITY: Census Bureau reports are available for purchase by all interested persons.

HOW TO APPLY: No application is necessary.

FOR MORE INFORMATION: Data User Services Office
Bureau of the Census
Washington, D.C. 20233

NOTE: *Census Bureau publications are also available in most libraries.*

RELATED PROGRAMS: Census Maps

UNIFORM CRIME REPORTS

PROGRAM: Do you want to know some *facts* about the crime problem?

The FBI collects, analyzes and publishes certain crime statistics which it receives on a regular and voluntary basis from law enforcement agencies nationwide. This data is published annually in "Crime in the United States—Uniform Crime Reports" and is supplemented with quarterly releases. Both the annual publication and the releases provide information on (1) crime trends; (2) offenses known to police; (3) age, sex and race of persons arrested; (4) police disposition of persons arrested; (5) police employee information; and (6) data concerning certain criminal career studies.

ELIGIBILITY: Limited copies are available to any interested individual.

HOW TO APPLY: Inquiries may be sent to the address below.

FOR MORE INFORMATION: Director
Federal Bureau of Investigation
Department of Justice
Washington, D.C. 20535

RELATED PROGRAMS: None

APPENDIX – Agency Addresses

DEPARTMENT OF AGRICULTURE

Agricultural Stabilization and Conservation Service

Alabama
P.O. Box 891 (for letter mail), or Rm. 714, 474 South Court St., Montgomery, Ala. 36102
(205) 265-5617

Alaska
Rm. 325, 308 G St., Anchorage, Alaska 99501
(907) 277-7659

Arizona
Rm. 6016, Federal Bldg, 230 North First Ave., Phoenix, Ariz, 85025
(602) 261-3261

Arkansas
P.O. Box 2781 (for letter mail), or Rm. 5416, New Federal Bldg, 700 West Capitol St., Little Rock, Ark. 72203
(501) 378-5220

California
2020 Milvia St., Berkeley, Calif, 94704
(415) 841-5121

Colorado
Rm.. 219, 2490 West 26th Ave., Denver, Colo. 80202
(303) 297-4611

Connecticut
Rm. 307-B, Post Office Bldg, 135 High St., Hartford, Conn. 06101
(203) 244-3310

Delaware
1722 Faulkland Road, Wilmington, Del. 19805
(302) 999-0188

Florida
P.O. Drawer 670 (for letter mail), or U.S. Federal Bldg, 401 S.E. First Ave., Gainesville, Fla. 32601
(904) 327-8549

Georgia
Beachwood Office Bldg, P.O. Box 5518, Athens, Ga. 30604
(404) 543-9642

Hawaii
Rm. 417, 1833 Kalakaua Ave., Honolulu, Hawaii 96815
(808) 955-0468

Idaho
Rm. 149, 304 North 8th St., Boise, Idaho 83702
(208) 342-2711, Ext. 248

Illinois
Rm. 232, U.S. Post Office and Courthouse, Springfield, Ill. 62701
(217) 525-4180

Indiana
Suite 1600, 5610 Crawfordsville Rd., Indianapolis, Ind. 46224
(317) 633-8521

Iowa
Rm. 937, Federal Bldg., 210 Walnut St., Des Moines, Iowa 50309
(515) 284-4213

Kansas
2601 Anderson Ave., Manhattan, Kans. 66502
(913) 539-3531

Kentucky
Imperial Towers Bldg., 333 Waller Ave., Lexington, Ky. 40504
(606) 252-2312

Louisiana
3737 Government St., Alexandria, La. 71301
(318) 443-9753

Maine
USDA Office Bldgs., University of Maine, Orono, Maine 04473
(207) 866–4976

Maryland
Rm. 420, Hartwick Bldg., 4321 Hartwick Rd., College Park, Md. 20740
(202) 388–8893

Massachusetts
P.O. Box 609 (for letter mail) or 29 Cottage St., Amherst, Mass. 01002
(413) 549–0540

Michigan
Room 116, 1405 South Harrison Rd., East Lansing, Mich. 48823
(517) 337–9436

Minnesota
Rm. 230, Federal Bldg. and U.S. Courthouse, 316 Robert St., St. Paul, Minn. 55101
(612) 725–7651

Mississippi
420 Milner Bldg., 200 South Lamar St. or P.O. Box 1251 (for letter mail), Jackson, Miss. 39205
(601) 948–7821. Ext. 231

Missouri
I.O.O.F. Bldg., 10th and Walnut Sts., Columbia, Mo. 65201
(314) 442–2271, Ext. 3113

Montana
P.O. Box 670 (for letter mail) or U.S. Post Office and Federal Bldg., Bozeman, Mont. 59715
(406) 587–4511

Nebraska
P.O. Box 82208 (for letter mail) or 5801 O St., Lincoln, Nebr. 68501
(402) 475–3361

Nevada
P.O. Box 360 (for letter mail) or Rm. 222 U.S. Post Office Bldg., S. Va. and Mill Sts., Reno, Nev. 89504
(702) 784–5411

New Hampshire
P.O. Box E (for letter mail) or Room 205, Federal Bldg., Durham, N.H. 03824
(603) 868–5582

New Jersey
P.O. Box 188 (for letter mail) or 1370 Hamilton St., Somerset, N.J. 08873
(201) 846–4281

New Mexico
P.O. Box 1458 (for letter mail) or Room 4406, Federal Bldg., 517 Gold Ave. S.W., Albuquerque, N. Mex. 87103
(505) 843–2472

New York
416 Midtown Plaza, 700 East Water St., Syracuse, N.Y. 13210
(315) 473–2644

North Carolina
P.O. Box 27327 (for letter mail) or Rm. 658, Federal Bldg., 310 New Bern Ave., Raleigh, N.C. 27601
(919) 755–4385

North Dakota
P.O. Box 3046 (for letter mail) or 657 Second Ave., N., Fargo, N. Dak. 58102
(701) 237–5771

Ohio
Rm. 116, Old Federal Bldg., Columbus, Ohio 43215
(614) 469–6735

Oklahoma
Agriculture Center, Office Bldg., Stillwater, Okla. 74074
(405) 372–7111

Oregon
1218 S.W. Wash. St., Portland, Oreg. 97205
(503) 221–2741

Pennsylvania
P.O. Box 1004 (for letter mail) or Federal Courthouse Bld., 228 Walnut St., Harrisburg, Pa. 17108
(717) 782–4547

Rhode Island
Rm. 506, Federal Bldg. and U.S. Court House, Kennedy Plaza, Providence, R.I. 02903
(401) 528–4301

South Carolina
P.O. Box 970 (for letter mail) or 7th Floor, Federal Office Bldg., 901 Sumter St., Columbia, S.C. 29202
(803) 765–5186

South Dakota
P.O. Box 843 (for letter mail) or 239 Wisconsin Ave., S.W., Huron, S. Dak. 57350
(605) 325–8651, Ext. 325

Tennessee
Rm. 579, U.S. Courthouse, Nashville, Tenn. 37203
(615) 749–5555

Texas
USDA Bldg., College Station, Tex. 77840
(713) 846–8821

Utah
Rm. 4239, 125 South State St., Salt Lake City, Utah 84111
(801) 524–5013

Vermont
151 South Prospect St., Burlington, Vt. 05401
(802) 862–6386

Virginia
Federal Bldg., 400 North 8th St., Richmond, Va. 23240

Washington
Rm. 391, U.S. Courthouse, 920 West Riverside, Spokane, Wash. 99201
(509) 456–3848

West Virginia
P.O. Box 1049 (for letter mail) or 209 Prairie Ave., Morgantown, W. Va. 26505
(304) 599–7351

Wisconsin
P.O. Box 4248 (for letter mail) or 4601 Hammersley Rd., Madison, Wis. 53711
(608) 256–4441, Ext. 7535

Wyoming
P.O. Box 920 (for letter mail) or 100 East B St., Casper, Wyo. 82602
(307) 265–5550, Ext. 3231

Caribbean Area
P.O. Box 8037 (for letter mail), Fernandez Juncos Station, or 1409 Ponce de Leon Ave., Stop 20, Segarra Bldg, San Juan, P.R. 00910
(809) 723–2380

Farmers Home Administration

Alabama
Rm. 717, Aronov Bldg., 474 South Court St., Montgomery, Ala. 36104
(205) 265–5611, Ext. 302

Arizona
Rm. 6026, Federal Bldg., 230 North First Ave., Phoenix, Ariz. 85025
(602) 261–3191

Arkansas
P.O. Box 2778, Little Rock, Ark. 72203
(501) 378–5436

California (Nevada, Hawaii)
2020 Milvia St., Berkeley, Calif. 94704
(415) 841–5121, Ext. 296

Colorado
New Federal Bldg., Rm. 231, No. 1 Diamond Plaza, 2490 West 26th Ave., Denver, Colo. 80211
(303) 837-4347

Florida
P.O. Box 1088, Gainesville, Fla. 32601
(904) 376-1681

Georgia
Suite 900, Peachtree 25th Bldg., 1720 Peachtree St., N.W., Atlanta, Ga. 20309
(404) 526-3924

Idaho
Rm. 418, Federal Bldg., 304 N. Eighth St., Boise, Idaho 83702
(208) 342-2711

Illinois
14 Federal Bldg., Champaign, Ill. 61820
(217) 356-1891

Indiana
Suite 1700, 5610 Crawfordsville, Rd., Indianpolis, Ind. 46224
(317) 633-8481

Iowa
873 Federal Bldg., 210 Walnut St., Des Moines, Iowa 50309
(515) 284-4121

Kansas
Rm. 630, New England Bldg., Fifth and Kansas, Topeka, Kans. 66603
(913) 234-8661, Ext. 375

Kentucky
1409 Forbes Rd., Lexington, Ky. 40505
(606) 252-2312, Ext. 2733

Louisiana
3727 Government St., Alexandria, La. 71301
(318) 443-7391

Maine
USDA Office Bldg., Orono, Maine 04472
(207) 866-4929

Michigan
1405 South Harrison Rd., East Lansing, Mich. 48823
(517) 372-1910, Ext. 272

Minnesota
U.S. Courthouse, 252 Federal Office Bldg., St. Paul, Minn. 55101
(612) 725-7695

Mississippi
Rm. 528, Milner Bldg., Jackson, Miss. 39201
(601) 948-7821, Ext. 372

Missouri
Parkade Plaza, Terrace Level, Columbia, Mo. 65201
(314) 442-2271, Ext. 3168

Montana
P.O. Box 350, Bozeman, Mont. 59715
(406) 587-4511

Nebraska
Rm. 430, Federal Bldg. and Courthouse, 129 North 10th St., Lincoln, Nebr. 68508
(402) 475-3342

New Jersey (Delaware, District of Columbia, Maryland)
P.O. Box 1478, Trenton, N.J. 08607
(609) 599-3511, Ext. 208

New Mexico
Rm. 3414, Federal Bldg., 517 Gold Ave. S.W. Albuquerque, N. Mex. 87101
(505) 843-0311, Ext. 2462

New York-
Rm. 203, Midtown Plaza, 700 East Water St., Syracuse, N.Y. 13210
(315) 473-3458

North Carolina
Rm. 514, Federal Bldg., 310 New Bern Ave., Raleigh, N.C. 27611
(919) 755-4640

North Dakota
Second Floor, Federal Bldg., Third and Rosser, Bismarck, N. Dak. 58502
(707) 255-4011, Ext. 4237

Ohio
Rm. 316, Old Post Office Bldg., Columbus, Ohio 43215
(614) 469-5606

APPENDIX

Oklahoma
Agricultural Center Office Bldg., Farm Rd., Stillwater, Okla. 74074
(405) 372-7111, Ext. 239

Oregon (Alaska)
1218 S.W., Washington St., Portland, Oreg. 97205
(503) 221-2731

Pennsylvania
Federal Bldg., 228 Walnut St., P.O. Box 905, Harrisburg, Pa. 17101
(717) 782-4476

Puerto Rico (Virgin Islands)
P.O. Box 4269, San Juan, P.R. 00905
722-3508

South Carolina
Federal Office Bldg., 901 Sumter St., Columbia, S.C. 29201
(803) 253-8371, Ext. 3350

South Dakota
P.O. Box 821, Huron, S. Dak. 57350
(605) 352-8651, Ext. 331

Tennessee
538 U.S. Court House Bldg., 801 Broadway, Nashville, Tenn. 37203
(615) 242-8321, Ext. 5501

Texas
3910 South General Bruce Drive, Temple, Tex. 76501
(817) 773-1711

Utah
Rm. 5311, Federal Bldg., 125 South State St., Salt Lake City, Utah 84111
(801) 524-5027

Vermont (Connecticut, Massachusetts, New Hampshire, Rhode Island)
3 West St., P.O. Box 588, Montpelier, Vt. 05602
(802) 229-9331

Virginia
P.O. Box 10106, Richmond, Va. 23240
(703) 782-2453

Washington
127 South Mission St., Wenatchee, Wash. 98801
(509) 662-5161

West Virginia
P.O. Box 678, Morgantown, W. Va. 26505
(304) 599-7256

Wisconsin
P.O. Box 4248, Madison, Wis. 53711
(608) 256-4441, Ext. 7551

Wyoming
P.O. Box 820, Casper, Wyo. 82601
(307) 265-5550, Ext. 3272

DEPARTMENT OF COMMERCE
Domestic and International Business Field Offices

Alabama
908 South 20th St., Suite 200-201, Birmingham, Ala., 35205
(205) 325-3327

Alaska
412 Hill Bldg., 632 Sixth St., Anchorage, Alaska 99501
(907) 272-6531

Arizona
5413 New Federal Bldg., 230 North First Ave., Phoenix, Ariz. 85025
(602) 261-3285

Arkansas
(See Tennessee)

California
Federal Office Bldg., 11th Floor, 11000 Wilshire Blvd., Los Angeles, Calif. 90024
(213) 824–7291

Federal Bldg., Box 36013, 450 Golden Gate Ave., San Francisco, Calif. 94102
(415) 556–5864

Colorado
New Customhouse, 19th and Stout Sts., Denver, Colo. 80202
(303) 297–3246

Connecticut
610 B Federal Office Bldg., 450 Main St., Hartford, Conn. 06103
(203) 244–3530

Delaware
(see Pennsylvania)

District of Columbia
(see Maryland)

Florida
City National Bank Bldg., Rm. 821, 25 West Flagler St., Miami, Fla. 33130
(305) 350–5267

P.O. Box 35087, 400 West Bay St., Jacksonville, Fla. 32202
(904) 791–2796

Georgia
235 U.S. Courthouse and Post Office Bldg., 152–29 Bull St., Savannah, Ga. 31402
(912) 232–4224

Suite 523, 1401 Peachtree St., N.E., Atlanta, Ga. 30309
(404) 526–6000

Hawaii
286 Alexander Young Bldg., 1015 Bishop St., Honolulu, Hawaii 96813
(808) 546–8694

Idaho
(see Washington, Oregon or Utah, nearest office)

Illinois
(see Chicago office below, or St. Louis, Mo., office if closer)

1486 New Federal Bldg., 219 South Dearborn St., Chicago, Ill. 60604
(312) 353–4450

Indiana
(see closest office; Cincinnati, Ohio, St. Louis, Mo. or Chicago, Ill.)

Iowa
609 Federal Bldg., 210 Walnut St., Des Moines, Iowa 50309
(515) 284–4222

Kansas
(see Kansas City, Mo.)

Kentucky
(see closest office; St. Louis or Cincinnati)

Louisiana
909 Federal Office Bldg. South, 610 South St., New Orleans, La. 70130
(504) 527–6546

Maine
(see Massachusetts)

Maryland
415 U.S. Customhouse, Gay and Lombard Sts., Baltimore, Md. 21202
(301) 962–3560

Massachusetts
441 Stuart St., Boston, Mass. 02116
(617) 223–2312

Michigan
445 Federal Bldg., Detroit, Mich. 48226
(313) 226–6063

Minnesota
306 Federal Bldg., 110 South Fourth St., Minneapolis, Minn. 55401
(612) 725–2133

Mississippi
(see closest office; Memphis or New Orleans)

Missouri
Rm. 1840, 601 East 12th St., Kansas City, Mo. 64106
(816) 374–3142

2511 Federal Bldg., 1520 Market St., St. Louis, Mo. 63103
(314) 622-4241

Montana
(see Washington)

Nebraska
(see nearest office; Cheyenne, Wyo., or Kansas City, Mo.)

Nevada
2028 Federal Bldg., 300 Booth St., Reno, Nev. 89502
(702) 784-5203

New Hampshire
(see Massachusetts)

New Jersey
(see nearest office; Philadnelphia or New York City)

New Mexico
U.S. Courthouse, Albuquerque, N. Mex. 87101
(505) 843-2386

New York
910 Federal Bldg., 111 West Huron St., Buffalo, N.Y. 14202
(716) 842-3208

Federal Office Bldg., 41st Floor, 26 Federal Plaza, Foley Square, New York, N.Y. 10007
(212) 264-0634

90 Church St., New York, N.Y. 10007
(212) 264-7594

North Carolina
258 Federal Bldg., West Market St., P.O. Box 1950, Greensboro, N.C. 27402
(919) 275-9345

North Dakota
(see Minnesota)

Ohio
8028 Federal Office Bldg., 550 Main St., Cincinnati, Ohio 45202
(513) 684-2944

Rm. 600, 666 Euclid Ave., Cleveland, Ohio 44114
(216) 522-4750

Oklahoma
(see Texas)

Oregon
Suite 501, 921 S.W. Morrison St., Portland, Oreg. 97204
(503) 226-3361

Pennsylvania
431 Federal Bldg., 1000 Liberty Ave., Pittsburgh, Pa. 15222
(412) 644-2850

Jefferson Bldg., 1015 Chestnut St., Philadelphia, Pa. 19107
(215) 597-2850

Puerto Rico
Rm. 100 Post Office Bldg., San Juan, P.R. 00902
(809) 723-4640

Rhode Island
(see Massachusetts)

South Carolina
Federal Bldg., Suite 631, 334 Meeting St., Charleston, S.C. 29403
(803) 577-4361

South Dakota
(see Minnesota)

Tennessee
Rm. 710, 147 Jefferson Ave., Memphis, Tenn. 38103
(901) 534-3214

Texas
1017 Old Federal Bldg., 201 Fannin St., Houston, Tex. 77002
(713) 226-4231

Room 3E7, 1100 Commerce St., Dallas, Tex. 75202
(214) 749-3287

Utah
1201 Federal Bldg., 125 South State St., Salt Lake City, Utah 84111
(801) 524-5116

Vermont
(see Massachusetts)

Virginia
2105 Federal Bldg., 400 North Eighth St., Richmond, Va. 23240
(703) 772–2240

Washington
8021 Federal Office Bldg., 909 First Ave., Seattle, Wash. 98104
(206) 583–5615

West Virginia
3000 New Federal Office Bldg., 500 Quarrier St., Charleston, W. Va. 25301
(304) 343–6181

Wisconsin
Straus Bldg., 238 West Wisconsin Ave., Milwaukee, Wis. 53203
(414) 224–3473

Wyoming
6022 O'Mahoney, Federal Center, 2120 Capitol Ave., Cheyenne, Wyo. 82001
(307) 778–2220, Ext. 2151

DEPARTMENT OF HEALTH, EDUCATION, AND WELFARE
REGIONAL OFFICES

Region 1 (Connecticut, Maine, Massachusetts, New Hampshire, Rhode Island, Vermont)
John F. Kennedy Federal Bldg., Government Center, Boston, Mass. 02203
(617) 223–6831

Region 2 (New York, New Jersey, Puerto Rico, the Virgin Islands)
26 Federal Plaza, New York, N.Y. 10007
(212) 264–4600

Region 3 (Delaware, District of Columbia, Maryland, Pennsylvania, Virginia, West Virginia)
401 North Broad St., Philadelphia, Pa. 19108
(215) 597–9050

Region 4 (Alabama, Florida, Georgia, Kentucky, Mississippi, North Carolina, South Carolina, Tennessee)
50 Seventh St., N.E., Rm. 404, Atlanta, Ga. 30323
(404) 526–5817

Region 5 (Illinois, Indiana, Minnesota, Michigan, Ohio, Wisconsin) 300 South Wacker Dr., Chicago, Ill. 60607
(312) 353–5160

Region 6 (Arkansas, Louisiana, New Mexico, Oklahoma, Texas) 1114 Commerce St., Dallas, Tex. 75202
(214) 749–3396

Region 7 (Iowa, Kansas, Missouri, and Nebraska) 601 East 12th St., Kansas City, Mo. 64106
(816) 374–3436

Region 8 (Colorado, Montana, North Dakota, South Dakota, Utah, Wyoming)
9017 Federal Office Bldg., 19th and Stout Sts., Denver, Colo. 80202
(303) 837–3373

Region 9 (Arizona, California, Hawaii, Nevada, Guam, American Samoa, Wake Island, Trust Territories of the Pacific Islands)
Federal Office Bldg., 50 Fulton St., San Francisco, Calif. 94102
(415) 556–6746

Region 10 (Alaska, Idaho, Oregon, Washington)
1312 Second Ave., Seattle, Wash. 98101
(206) 442–0421

APPENDIX

Food and Drug Administration
DISTRICT OFFICES

California
1521 West Pico Blvd., Los Angeles, Calif.
90015
(213) 688–3771

Federal Office Bldg., 50 Fulton St., Rm.
518 San Francisco, Calif. 94102
(415) 556–2062

Colorado
513 New Customhouse Bldg., 20th and
California Sts., Denver, Colo. 80202
(303) 297–4335

Georgia
60 Eighth Street, N.E., Atlanta, Ga. 30309
(404) 526–5265

Illinois
Main Post Office Bldg., Rm. 1222, 433 West
Van Buren St., Chicago, Ill. 60607
(312) 353–5863

Louisiana
U.S. Customhouse Bldg., Rm. 222, 423
Canal St., New Orleans, La. 70130
(504) 527–2401

Maryland
900 Madison Ave., Baltimore, Md. 21201
(301) 962–4056

Massachusetts
585 Commercial St., Boston, Mass. 02109
(617) 223–3171

Michigan
1560 East Jefferson Ave., Detroit, Mich.
48207
(313) 226–6262

Minnesota
240 Hennepin Ave., Minneapolis, Minn.
55401
(612) 725–2121

Missouri
1009 Cherry St., Kansas City, Mo. 64106
(816) 374–5521

New York
850 3rd Ave., Rm. 700, Brooklyn, N.Y.
11232
(212) 788–1300

599 Delaware Ave., Buffalo, N.Y. 14202
(716) 842–3311

Ohio
1141 Central Parkway, Cincinnati, Ohio
45202
(513) 684–3508

Pennsylvania
Rm. 1204, U.S. Customhouse. Second and
Chestnut Sts., Philadelphia, Pa. 19106
(215) 597–4391

Texas
3032 Bryan St., Dallas, Tex. 75204
(214) 749–2733

Washington
Federal Office Bldg., 909 First Ave., Rm.
501, Seattle, Wash., 98104
(206) 583–5300

SOCIAL SECURITY OFFICES

Social Security offices are located in the cities listed below. To find the address of the office in one of these cities, consult the Telephone Directory under Social Security Administration or U.S. Government, or ask at your post office.

Alabama
Andalusia, Anniston, Bessemer, Birmingham, Cullman, Decatur, Dothan, Florence, Gadsden, Huntsville, Jasper, Mobile, Montgomery, Opelika, Selma, Talladega, Tuscaloosa

Alaska
Anchorage, Fairbanks, Juneau, Ketchikan

American Samoa
Pago Pago

Arizona
Bisbee, Casa Grande, Flagstaff, Glendale, Globe, Mesa , Phoenix, Prescott, Safford, Scottsdale, South Tucson , Tucson, Yuma

Arkansas
Batesville, Blytheville, Camden, El Dorado, Fayetteville, Forrest City, Fort Smith, Helena, Hot Springs National Park, Jonesboro, Little Rock, Pine Bluff, Russellville, Searcy, West Memphis

California
Anaheim, Bakersfield, Berkeley, Bishop, Canoga Park, Chico, Chula Vista, Compton, Crescent City, Delano , East Los Angeles, El Cajon, El Centro, El Monte, El Sereno, Escondido, Eureka, Fresno, Gilroy, Glendale, Hayward, Hemet, Hollywood, Huntington Park, Inglewood, Lancaster, Long Beach, Los Angeles, Madera , Marysville, Merced, Modesto, Monterey, Monterey Park, Norwalk, Oakland, Oceanside, Palm Springs, Palo Alto, Pasadena, Pomona, Porterville, Redding, Richmond, Riverside, Sacramento, Salinas, San Bernardino, San Diego, San Fernando, San Francisco, San Jose, San Luis Obispo, San Mateo, San Rafael, Santa Ana, Santa Barbara, Santa Cruz, Santa Maria, Santa Monica, Santa Rosa, Sonora, Stockton, Susanville, Torrance, Ukiah, Vallejo, Van Nuys, Ventura, Visalia, Walnut Creek, Watsonville, West Covina, Whittier

Colorado
Alamosa, Boulder, Colorado Springs, Denver, Durango, Englewood, Fort Collins, Glenwood Springs, Grand Junction, Greeley, La Junta, Lakewood, Pueblo, Sterling, Trinidad

Connecticut
Ansonia, Bridgeport, Danbury, East Bridgeport, East Hartford, Hartford, Meriden, New Britain, New Haven, New London, Stamford, Torrington, Waterbury, Willimantic

Delaware
Dover, Wilmington

District of Columbia
Washington

Florida
Bradenton, Clearwater, Coral Gables, Cutler Ridge, Daytona Beach, Deland, Fort Lauderdale, Fort Myers, Fort Pierce, Gainesville, Hialeah, Holiday, Hollywood, Jacksonville, Key West, Lake City, Lakeland, Leesburg, Melbourne, Miami, Miami Beach, North Miami, Ocala, Orlando, Panama City, Pensacola, Plant City, Pompano Beach, Sanford, Sarasota, St. Augustine, St. Petersburg, Tallahassee, Tampa, West Palm Beach, Winter Haven

Georgia
Albany, Athens, Atlanta, Augusta, Brunswick, Columbus, Dalton, Decatur, Dublin, East Point, Gainesville, Griffin, La Grange, Macon, Marietta, Rome, Savannah, Thomasville, Valdosta, Waycross

Guam
Agana

Hawaii
Hilo, Honolulu, Lihue, Wailuku, Waipahu

Idaho
Boise, Caldwell, Coeur d'Alene, Idaho Falls, Lewiston, Pocatello, Twin Falls

Illinois
Alton, Arlington Heights, Aurora, Berwyn, Bloomington, Cairo, Carbondale, Champaign, Chicago, Danville, Decatur, Des Plaines, East St. Louis, Effingham, Elgin, Elmwood Park, Evanston, Freeport, Galesburg, Glenview, Harrisburg, Harvey, Joliet, Kankakee, Mount Vernon, Peoria, Pekin, Peru, Quincy, Rockford, Rock Island, Springfield, Sterling, Villa Park, Waukegan, Woodstock.

Indiana
Anderson, Bloomington, Columbus, Crawfordsville, East Chicago, Elkhart, Evansville, Fort Wayne, Gary, Hammond, Indianapolis, Kokomo, Lafayette, Madison, Marion, Michigan City, Muncie, New Albany, Richmond, South Bend, Terre Haute, Valparaiso, Vincennes.

APPENDIX

Iowa
Burlington, Cedar Rapids, Creston, Davenport, Des Moines, Dubuque, Fort Dodge, Mason City, Ottumwa, Sioux City, Waterloo

Kansas
Colby, Dodge City, Hays, Hutchinson, Independence, Kansas City, Liberal, Manhattan, Pittsburg, Salina, Shawnee Mission, Topeka, Wichita

Kentucky
Ashland, Bowling Green, Campbellsville, Corbin, Covington, Danville, Elizabethtown, Frankfort, Harlan, Hazard, Hopkinsville, Lexington, Louisville, Madisonville, Maysville, Middleboro, Owensboro, Paducah, Pikeville, Somerset

Louisiana
Alexandria, Baton Rouge, Bogalusa, Hammond, Houma, Lafayette, Lake Charles, Metaire, Montor, Morgan City, Natchitoches, New Orleans, Opelousas, Shreveport

Maine
Augusta, Bangor, Biddeford, Lewiston, Portland, Presque Isle, Rockland

Maryland
Baltimore, Bel Air, Cambridge, Camp Springs, Catonsville, Cumberland, Elkton, Frederick, Glen Burnie, Hagerstown, Pikesville, Rockville, Salisbury, Silver Spring, Towson

Massachusetts
Attleboro, Boston, Brockton, Cambridge, Chelsea, Dorchester, Fall River, Fitchburg, Framingham, Greenfield, Haverhill, Holyoke, Hyannis, Lawrence, Lowell, Lynn, Malden, New Bedford, Norwood, Pittsfield, Quincy, Roslindale, Roxbury, Salem, Springfield, Taunton, Waltham, Worcester

Michigan
Alpena, Ann Arbor, Bad Axe, Battle Creek, Bay City, Benton Harbor, Dearborn, Detroit, Escanaba, Flint, Grand Rapids, Highland Park, Houghton, Iron Mountain, Ironwood, Jackson, Kalamazoo, Lansing, Marquette, Monroe, Mount Pleasant, Muskegon, Petoskey, Pontiac, Port Huron, Roseville, Royal Oak, Saginaw, Sault Sainte Marie, Traverse City

Minnesota
Austin, Bemidji, Brainerd, Duluth, Fairmont, Hibbing, Mankato, Marshall, Minneapolis, Rochester, St. Cloud, St. Paul, Winona

Mississippi
Clarksdale, Columbus, Greenville, Greenwood, Gulfport, Hattiesburg, Jackson, Laurel, McComb, Meridian, Natchez, Pascagoula, Philadelphia, Tupelo, Vicksburg

Missouri
Cape Girardeau, Chillicothe, Clayton, Columbia, Flat River, Hannibal, Independence, Jefferson City, Joplin, Kansas City, Kennett, Moberly, Poplar Bluff, Rolla, St. Joseph, St. Louis, Sedalia, Springfield, West Plains

Montana
Billings, Bozeman, Butte, Glasgow, Great Falls, Havre, Helena, Kalispell, Miles City, Missoula

Nebraska
Beatrice, Grand Island, Hastings, Lincoln, Norfolk, North Platte, Omaha, Scottsbluff

Nevada
Elko, Las Vegas, Reno

New Hampshire
Concord, Keene, Littleton, Manchester, Nashua, Portsmouth

New Jersey
Asbury Park, Atlantic City, Bloomfield, Bridgeton, Camden, East Orange, Elizabeth, Hackensack, Irvington, Jersey City, Morristown, Newark, New Brunswick, Passaic, Paterson, Perth Amboy, Plainfield, Trenton, Wildwood

New Mexico
Albuquerque, Clovis, Farmington, Gallup, Hobbs, Las Cruces, Roswell, Santa Fe

New York
Albany, Auburn, Batavia, Binghamton, Bronx, Brooklyn, Buffalo, Corning, Elmira, Far Rockaway, Flushing, Freeport, Geneva, Glens Falls, Gloversville, Hudson, Huntington, Ithaca, Jackson Heights, Jamaica,

Jamestown, Kenmore, Kingston, Mineola, Monticello, New City, New Rochelle, New York City (Manhattan), Newburgh, Niagara Falls, Ogdensburg, Olean, Oneonta, Oswego, Patchogue, Plattsburgh, Poughkeepsie, Riverhead, Rochester, Rome, Schenectady, Staten Island, Syracuse, Troy, Utica, Watertown, White Plains, Yonkers

North Carolina
Albermarle, Asheville, Burlington, Charlotte, Durham, Elizabeth City, Fayetteville, Gastonia, Goldsboro, Greensboro, Greenville, Hickory, High Point, Kannapolis, Kinston, Lumberton, New Bern, North Wilkesboro, Raleigh, Roanoke Rapids, Rockingham, Rocky Mount, Salisbury, Statesville, Wilmington, Winston-Salem.

North Dakota
Bismarck, Fargo, Grand Forks, Minot, Williston

Ohio
Akron, Ashtabula, Canton, Chillicothe, Cincinnati, Cleveland, Columbus, Dayton, Defiance, East Liverpool, Findlay, Hamilton, Ironton, Lancaster, Lima, Lorain, Mansfield, Marietta, Marion, Middletown, New Philadelphia, Newark, Prama, Painesville, Piqua, Portsmouth, Sandusky, Springfield, Steubenville, Toledo, Warren, Wooster, Youngstown, Zanesville

Oklahoma
Ada, Altus, Ardmore, Bartlesville, Clinton, Enid, Lawton, McAlester, Miami, Muskogee, Norman, Oklahoma City, Ponca City, Shawnee, Tulsa

Oregon
Astoria, Beaverton, Bend, Coos Bay, Eugene, Klamath Falls, La Grande, Medford, Ontario, Pendleton, Portland, Roseburg, Salem, The Dalles

Pennsylvania
Allentown, Altoona, Ambridge, Beaver Falls, Bloomsburg, Braddock, Bristol, Butler, Chambersburg, Charleroi, Chester, Du Bois, Easton, Erie, Greensburg, Harrisburg, Hazleton, Indiana, Johnstown, Lancaster, Lebanon, Meadville, McKeesport, New Castle, New Kensington, Norristown, Oil City, Philadelphia, Pittsburgh, Pittstown, Pottsville, Reading, Scranton, Sharon, State College, Sunbury, Uniontown, Upper Darby, Washington, West Chester, Wilkes-Barre, Williamsport, York

Puerto Rico
Agaudilla, Arecibo, Bayamon, Caguas, Humacao, Mayaguez, Ponce, San Juan

Rhode Island
Pawtucket, Providence, Warwick, Woonsocket

South Carolina
Aiken, Anderson, Bennettsville, Charleston, Columbia, Conway, Florence, Georgetown, Greenville, Greenwood, Orangeburg, Rock Hill, Spartanburg, Sumter

South Dakota
Aberdeen, Huron, Pierre, Rapid City, Sioux Falls, Watertown

Tennessee
Chattanooga, Clarksville, Cleveland, Columbia, Cookeville, Dyersburg, East Memphis, Greeneville, Jackson, Johnson City, Kingsport, Knoxville, La Follette, Maryville, Memphis, Morristown, Murfreesboro, Nashville, Paris, Tullahoma

Texas
Abilene, Alice, Amarillo, Austin, Beaumont, Big Spring, Brownsville, Brownwood, Bryan, Corpus Christi, Corsicana, Dallas, Denton, Eagle Pass, El Paso, Fort Worth, Galveston, Greenville, Harlinge, Houston, Huntsville, Kerrville, Laredo, Longview, Lubbock, Lufkin, Marshall, McAllen, McKinney, Odessa, Palestine, Pampa, Paris, Pasadena, Plainview, Port Auther, San Angelo, San Antonio, Sherman Temple, Texarkana, Tyler, Vernon, Victoria, Waco, Wichita Falls

Utah
Cedar City, Ogden, Provo, Salt Lake City

APPENDIX

Vermont
Burlington, Montpelier, Rutland

Virginia
Alexandria, Arlington, Bristol, Charlottesville, Covington, Danville, Falls Church, Farmville, Lynchburg, Martinsville, Newport News, Norfolk, Norton, Petersburg, Portsmouth, Richmond, Roanoke, South Boston, Stanton, Winchester, Wytheville

Virgin Islands
Christiansted, St. Thomas

Washington
Aberdeen, Bellevue, Bellingham, Bremerton, Everett, Longview, Okanagan, Olympia, Pasco, Port Angeles, Renton, Seattle, Spokane, Tacoma, Vancouver, Walla Walla, Wenatchee, Yakima

West Virginia
Beckley, Bluefield, Charleston, Clarksburg, Elkins, Fairmont, Huntington, Logan, Martinsburg, Morgantown, Parkersburg, Welch, Wheeling

Wisconsin
Appleton, Eau Claire, Fond du Lac, Green Bay, Janesville, Kenosha, La Crosse, Lancaster, Madison, Manitowoc, Marinette, Milwaukee, Oshkosh, Portage, Racine, Rhinelander, Sheboygan, South Milwaukee, Superior, Waukesha, Wausau, Wisconsin Rapids

Wyoming
Casper, Cheyenne, Cody, Riverton, Rock Spring, Sheridan, Worland

DEPARTMENT OF HOUSING AND URBAN DEVELOPMENT

Region 1 (Connecticut, Maine, Massachusetts, New Hampshire, Rhode Island, Vermont)

Boston Regional Office
800 John F. Kennedy Federal Bldg., Boston., Mass. 02203
(617) 223-4066

Boston Area Office (Massachusetts, Rhode Island)
Bulfinch Bldg., 15 New Chardon St., Boston, Mass. 02114
(617) 223-4111

Hartford Area Office (Connecticut)
999 Asylum Ave., Hartford, Conn. 06105
(203) 244-3638

Manchester Area Office (Main, New Hampshire, Vermont)
Davison Bldg., 1230 Elm St., Manchester, N.H. 03101
(603) 669-7681

Bangor Insuring Office (Maine)
Federal Bldg. and Post Office, 202 Harlow St., Bangor, Maine 04401
(207) 942-8271

Burlington Insuring Office (Vermont)
630 Federal Bldg., Elmwood Ave., Burlington, Vt. 05402
(802) 862-6274

Providence Insuring Office (Rhode Island) 300 Post Office Annex, Providence, R.I. 02903
(401) 528-4391

Region 2 (New York, New Jersey, Puerto Rico, Virgin Islands, Panama Canal Zone)

New York Regional Office
26 Federal Plaza, New York, N.Y. 10007
(212) 264-8068

Buffalo Area Office (western New York State)
Grant Bldg., 560 Main St., Buffalo, N.Y. 14202
(716) 842-3510

Camden Area Office (southern New Jersey) The Parkade Bldg., 519 Federal St., Camden, N.J. 08103
(609) 963-2301

Newark Area Office (northern New Jersey) Gateway 1 Bldg., Raymond Plaza, Newark, N.J. 07102
(201) 645-3010

New York Area Office (eastern New York State)
120 Church St., New York, N.Y. 10007
(212) 264-0522

San Juan, Commonwealth Area Office (Puerto Rico, Virgin Islands, Panama Canal Zone)
New Pan Am. Bldg., 255 Ponce de Leon Ave., Hato Rey, P.R.
Mailing Address: P.O. Box 3869, GPO, San Juan, P.R. 00936
(809) 622-0201

Albany Insuring Office (northern New York State)
30 Russell Rd., Westgate North, Albany, N.Y. 12206
(518) 472-3567

Hempstead Insuring Office (southern New York State)
175 Fulton Ave., Hempstead, N.Y. 11550
(516) 485-5000

Region 3 (Delaware, District of Columbia, Maryland, Pennsylvania, Virginia, West Virginia)

Philadelphia Regional Office
Curtis Bldg., 625 Walnut St., Philadelphia, Pa. 19106
(215) 597-2560

Baltimore Area Office (Maryland, except Montgomery and Prince Georges Counties)
Mercantile Bank and Trust Bldg., Two Hopkins Plaza, Baltimore, Md. 21201
(301) 962-2121

District of Columbia Area Office (District of Columbia, Montgomery and Prince Georges Counties in Maryland, and northern Virginia State)
Universal North Bldg., 1875 Connecticut Ave., N.W., Washington, D.C. 20009
(202) 382-5691

Philadelphia Area Office (eastern Pennsylvania, Delaware)
Curtis Bldg., 625 Walnut St., Philadelphia, Pa. 19106
(215) 597-2358

Pittsburgh Area Office (western Pennsylvania, West Virginia)
1000 Liberty Ave., Pittsburgh, Pa. 15222
(412) 644-2802

Richmond Area Office (southern Virginia State)
701 East Franklin St., P.O. Box 10011, Richmond, Va. 23240
(703) 782-2721

Charleston Insuring Office (West Virginia)
New Federal Bldg., 500 Quarrier St., Charleston, W. Va. 25301
Mailing address: P.O. Box 2948, Charleston, W. Va. 25330
(304) 343-6181

Wilmington Insuring Office (Delaware)
536 Wilmington Trust Bldg., Wilmington, Del. 19801
(302) 658-6911

Region 4 (Alabama, Florida, Georgia, Kentucky, Mississippi, North Carolina, South Carolina, Tennessee)

Atlanta Regional Office (Georgia)
Peachtree Seventh Bldg., 50 Seventh St., N.E., Atlanta, Ga. 30323
(404) 526-5585

Atlanta Area Office (Georgia)
1100 Peachtree Center Bldg., 230 Peachtree St., N.W., Atlanta, Ga. 30303
(404) 526-4576

Birmingham Area Office (Alabama)
Daniel Bldg., 15 South 20th St., Birmingham, Ala. 35233
(205) 325-3264

Columbia Area Office (South Carolina)
1801 Main St., Jefferson Square, Columbia, S.C. 29201
(803) 253-8371

Greensboro Area Office (North Carolina)
2309 West Cone Blvd., Northwest Plaza, Greensboro, N.C. 27408
(919) 275-9111

Jackson Area Office (Mississippi)
101-C Third Floor Jackson Mall, 300 Woodrow Wilson Ave., West, Jackson, Miss. 39213
(601) 948-7821

Jacksonville Area Office (Florida)
Peninsular Plaza, 661 Riverside Ave., Jacksonville, Fla. 32204
(904) 791-2626

Knoxville Area Office (Tennessee)
1 Northshore Bldg., 1111 Northshore Dr., Knoxville, Tenn. 37919
(615) 584-8527

Louisville Area Office (Kentucky)
Children's Hospital Foundation Bldg., 601 South Floyd St., Louisville, Ky. 40202
(502) 582-5254

Coral Gables Insuring Office (southern Florida State)
3001 Ponce de Leon Blvd., Coral Gables, Fla. 33134
(305) 445-2561

Memphis Insuring Office (western Tennessee State)
447 Federal Office Bldg., 167 N. Main St., Memphis, Tenn. 38103
(901) 534-3141

Nashville Insuring Office (central Tennessee State)
1717 West End Bldg., Nashville, Tenn. 37203
(615) 749-5521

Tampa Insuring Office (central Florida State)
4224-28 Henderson Blvd., P.O. Box 18165, Tampa, Fla. 33609
(813) 228-7711

Region 5 (Illinois, Indiana, Michigan, Minnesota, Ohio, Wisconsin)

Chicago Regional Office
300 South Wacker Dr., Chicago, Ill. 60606
(312) 353-5680

Chicago Area Office (Illinois)
17 N. Dearborn St., Chicago, Ill. 60602
(312) 353-7660

Columbia Area Office (Ohio)
60 East Main St., Columbus, Ohio 43215
(614) 469-5737

Detroit Area Office (Michigan)
5th Floor First National Bldg., 660 Woodward Ave., Detroit, Mich. 48226
(313) 226-7900

Indianapolis Area Office (Indiana)
Willowbrook 5 Bldg., 4720 Kingsway Dr., Indianapolis, Ind. 46205
(317) 633-7188

Milwaukee Area Office (Wisconsin)
744 North 4th St., Milwaukee, Wis. 53203
(414) 272-8600

Minneapolis-St. Paul Area Office (Minnesota
Griggs-Midway Bldg., 1821 University Ave., St. Paul, Minn., 55104
(612) 725-4801

Cincinnati Insuring Office (southwestern Ohio State)
9009 Federal Office Bldg., 550 Main St., Cincinnati, Ohio 45202
(513) 684-2884

Cleveland, Insuring Office (northern Ohio State)
907 Federal Bldg., 1240 East 9th St., Cleveland, Ohio 44199
(216) 522-4065

Grand Rapids Insuring Office (western and northern Michigan State)
921 North Division Ave., Grand Rapids, Mich. 49503
(616) 456-2225

Springfield Insuring Office (central and southern Illinois State)
Lincoln Tower Plaza, 542 South Second St., P.O. Box 1628, Springfield, Ill. 62705
(217) 525-4085

Region 6 (Arkansas, Louisiana, New Mexico, Oklahoma, Texas)

Fort Worth Regional Office
Federal Office Bldg., 819 Taylor St., Fort Worth, Tex. 76102
(817) 334-2867

Dallas Area Office (New Mexico, eastern, northern, and western Texas)
14-A-18 New Dallas Federal Bldg., 1100 Commerce St., Dallas, Tex. 75202
(214) 749-2158

Little Rock Area Office (Arkansas and Bowie County, Texas)
Union National Bank Bldg., One Union National Plaza, Little Rock, Ark. 72201
(501) 372-4361

New Orleans Area Office (Louisiana)
Plaza Tower, 1011 Howard Ave., New Orleans, La. 70113
(504) 527-2062

Oklahoma City Area Office (Oklahoma)
301 North Hudson St., Oklahoma City, Okla. 73102
(405) 231-4181

San Antonio Area Office (Southwest Texas)
Kallison Bldg., 410 South Main Ave., P.O. Box 9163, San Antonio, Tex. 78285
(512) 225-5511

Albuquerque Insuring Office (New Mexico)
625 Truman St. N.E., Albuquerque, N. Mex. 87110
(505) 256-9877

Fort Worth Insuring Office (north central Texas State)
9A35 Federal Bldg., 819 Taylor St., Fort Worth, Tex. 76102
(817) 334-3233

Houston Insuring Office (east central Texas State)
7419 Federal Bldg., 515 Rusk Ave., Houston, Tex. 77002
(713) 226-4335

Lubbock Insuring Office (northwest Texas State)
514 Courthouse and Federal Office Bldg., 1205 Texas Ave., Lubbock, Tex. 79401
(806) 747-3711

Shreveport Insuring Office northern Louisiana and 5 counties in eastern Texas)
Ricon-Brewster Bldg., 425 Milam St., Shreveport, La. 71101
(318) 425-1241

Tulsa Insuring Office (eastern Oklahoma State)
1708 Utica Square, P.O. Box 4054, Tulsa, Okla. 74152
(918) 584-7151

Region 7 (Iowa, Kansas, Missouri, Nebraska)

Kansas City Regional Office
322 Federal Office Bldg., 911 Walnut St., Kansas City, Mo. 64106
(816) 374-2661

Kansas City Area Office (Kansas, western Missouri)
One Gateway Center, 5th and State Sts., P.O. Box 1339, Kansas City, Kans. 66117
(816) 374-4355

Omaha Area Office (Iowa, Nebraska)
Univac Bldg., 7100 West Center Rd., Omaha, Nebr. 68106
(402) 221-4221

St. Louis Area Office (eastern Missouri)
210 North 12th St., St. Louis, Mo. 63101
(314) 622-4760

APPENDIX

Des Moines Insuring Office (Iowa)
259 Federal Bldg., 210 Walnut St., Des Moines, Iowa 50309
(515) 284-4481

Topeka Insuring Office (Kansas, except Johnson and Wyandotte counties)
700 Kansas Ave., Topeka, Kans. 66603
(913) 234-8241

Region 8 (Colorado, Montana, North Dakota, South Dakota, Utah, Wyoming)
Denver Regional Office
Federal Bldg., 1961 Stout St., Denver, Colo. 80202
(303) 837-4881

Casper Insuring Office (Wyoming)
Federal Office Bldg., 100 East B St., Casper, Wyo. 82601
(307) 265-4310

Denver Insuring Office (Colorado)
4th Floor Title Bldg., 909 17th St., Denver, Colo. 80202
(303) 837-4521

Fargo Insuring Office (North Dakota)
Federal Bldg., 653 2nd Ave. N., P.O. Box 2483, Fargo, N. Dak. 58102
(701) 237-5136

Helena Insuring Office (Montana)
616 Helena Ave., Helena, Mont. 59601
(406) 442-3237

Salt Lake City Insuring Office (Utah)
125 South State St., Salt Lake City, Utah 84111
(801) 524-5237

Sioux Falls Insuring Office (South Dakota) 119 Federal Bldg., U.S. Courthouse, 400 S. Phillips Ave., Sioux Falls, S. Dak. 57102
(605) 336-2980

Region 9 (Arizona, California, Hawaii, Nevada, Guam, American Samoa, Pacific Trust Territories)

San Francisco Regional Office
450 Golden Gate Ave., P.O. Box 36003, San Francisco, Calif. 94102
(415) 556-4752

Los Angeles Area Office (Arizona, southern California)
2500 Wilshire Blvd., Los Angeles, Calif., 90057
(213) 688-5127

San Francisco Area Office (northern California, Hawaii, Nevada, Guam, American Samoa, Pacific Trust Territories)
Suite 1600, 1 Embarcadero Center, San Francisco, Calif. 94111
(415) 556-2238

Honolulu Insuring Office (Hawaii, Guam, American Samoa
1000 Bishop St., P.O. Box 3377, Honolulu, Hawaii 96801
(808) 546-2136

Phoenix Insuring Office (Arizona)
244 W. Osborn Rd., P.O. Box 13468, Phoenix, Ariz. 85002
(609) 261-3900

Reno Insuring Office (Nevada)
70 Linden St., P.O. Box 4700, Reno, Nev. 89505
(702) 784-5213

Sacramento Insuring Office (northeastern California)
801 I St., P.O. Box 1978, Sacramento, Calif. 95809
(916) 449-3471

San Diego Insuring Office (Imperial and San Diego Counties, California)
110 West C St., P.O. Box 2648, San Diego, Calif. 92112
(714) 293-5310

Santa Ana Insuring Office (Orange, Riverside, and San Bernardino Counties, California, for home mortgages)
1440 East First St., Santa Ana, Calif. 92701
(714) 836-2451

Region 10 (Alaska, Idaho, Oregon, Washington)

Seattle Regional Office
Arcade Plaza Bldg., 1321 Second Ave., Seattle, Wash. 98101
(206) 442-5414

Portland Area Office (southern Idaho, Oregon, Washington Counties of Clark, Klickitat, and Skamania)
520 Southwest 6th Ave., Portland, Oreg. 97204
(503) 221–2558

Seattle Area Office (Alaska, northern Idaho, Washington except Clark, Klickitat, and Skamania Counties)
Arcade Plaza Bldg., 1321 Second Ave., Seattle, Wash. 98101
(206) 442–7456

Anchorage Insuring Office (Alaska)
228 Federal Bldg., P.O. Box 480, Anchorage, Alaska 99501
(907) 272–5561

Boise Insuring Office (westcentral Idaho, Baker and Malheur Counties in Oregon)
331 Idaho St., Boise, Idaho 83701
(208) 342–2711

Spokane Insuring Office (Northern Idaho, Eastern Washington)
920 Riverside Ave. West, Spokane, Wash. 99201
(509) 456–2510

DEPARTMENT OF THE INTERIOR
Bureau of Land Management
REGIONAL AND FIELD OFFICES

Alaska
555 Cordova St., Anchorage, Alaska 99501
(907) 277–1561

Arizona
Federal Bldg., Rm. 3022, Phoenix, Ariz., 85025
(602) 261–3873

California
Federal Office Bldg., Rm. E–2841, 2800 Cottage Way, Sacramento, Calif. 95825
(916) 481–2676

Colorado
Rm. 700, Colorado State Bank Bldg., 1600 Broadway, Denver, Colo. 80202
(303) 837–4325

Idaho
Rm. 334, Federal Bldg., 550 West Fort St., Boise, Idaho 83702
(208) 342–2401

Montana (North Dakota, South Dakota, Minnesota)
Federal Bldg., 316 North 26th St., Billings, Mont. 59101
(406) 245–6711

Nevada
Federal Bldg., Rm. 3008, 300 Booth St., Reno, Nev. 89502
(702) 784–5451

New Mexico (Oklahoma)
U.S. Post Office and Federal Bldg., South Federal Place, P.O. Box 1449, Santa Fe, N. Mex. 87501
(505) 982–3801

Oregon
729 Northeast Oregon St., P.O. Box 2965, Portland, Oreg. 97208
(503) 234–3361

Utah
Federal Bldg., 125 South State, P.O. Box 11505, Salt Lake City, Utah 84111
(801) 524–5311

Wyoming (Nebraska and Kansas)
U.S. Post Office and Court House Bldg., 2120 Capitol Ave., P.O. Box 1828, Cheyenne, Wyo. 82001
(307) 778–2326

Eastern States
7981 Eastern Ave., Silver Spring, Md. 20910. This office handles inquiries for Alabama, Florida, Louisiana, Michigan, Minnesota, Mississippi, Oklahoma, Wisconsin.
(301) 495–3200

APPENDIX

Bureau of Indian Affairs AREA OFFICES

[1] Cross-references denote which area office or offices provide services to eligible Indians within the State.

Alaska
Juneau Area Office, Box 3–8000, Juneau, Alaska 99801
(907) 586–7171

Arizona
Phoenix Area Office, 124 W. Thomas Rd., P.O. Box 7007, Phoenix, Ariz. 85011
(602) 261–4102

Navajo Area Office
P.O. Box 1060, Window Rock, Ariz. 86515
(602) 871–4368

California [1]
(See also Arizona (Phoenix))
Sacramento Area Office, Federal Office Bldg., 2800 Cottage Way, Sacramento, Calif. 95825
(916) 481–6100

Colorado [1] (See New Mexico)

District of Columbia
Southeast Agencies Director,
1951 Constitution Ave. N.W., Washington, D.C. 20242
(202) 343–5582

Commissioner of Indian Affairs,
1951 Constitution Ave. N.W., Washington, D.C. 20242
(202) 343–2111

Florida [1] (See District of Columbia (Southeast Agencies))

Idaho [1] (See Arizona (Phoenix) and Oregon)

Iowa [1] (See Minnesota)

Kansas [1] (See Oklahoma (Anadarko))

Louisiana [1] (See District of Columbia (Southeast Agencies))

Michigan [1] (See Minnesota)

Minnesota
Minneapolis Area Office, 831 Second Ave., S., Minneapolis, Minn. 55402
(612) 725–2904

Mississippi [1] (See District of Columbia (Southeast Agencies))

Montana
Billings Area Office, 316 North 26th St., Billings, Mont. 59101
(406) 245–6711

Nebraska [1] (See South Dakota)

Nevada [1] (See Arizona (Phoenix))

New Mexico [1] (See also Arizona (Navajo)) Albuquerque Area Office, 5301 Central Ave., Albuquerque, N. Mex. 87108
(505) 843–3173

New York [1] (See District of Columbia (Commissioner))

North Carolina [1] (See District of Columbia (Southeast Agencies))

North Dakota [1] (See South Dakota)

Oklahoma
Anadarko Area Office, Federal Bldg., P.O. Box 368, Anadarko, Okla. 73005
(405) 247–6673

Muskogee Area Office, Federal Bldg., Muskogee, Okla. 74401
(918) 683–3111

Oregon [1] (See also Arizona (Phoenix))
Portland Area Office, 1425 Irving St. N.E., P.O. Box 3785, Portland, Oreg. 97208
(503) 234–3361

South Dakota
Aberdeen Area Office, 820 South Main St., Aberdeen, S. Dak. 57401
(605) 225–0250

Utah [1] (See Arizona (Navajo and Phoenix) and Oregon)

Washington [1] (See Oregon)

Wisconsin [1] (See Minnesota)

Wyoming [1] (See Montana)

DEPARTMENT OF LABOR
Bureau of Labor Statistics
REGIONAL OFFICES

Region 1 (Connecticut, Maine, Massachusetts, New Hampshire, Rhode Island, Vermont)
Rm. 1603–B, Federal Office Bldg., Boston, Mass. 02203
(617) 223–6727

Region 2 (New Jersey, New York, Puerto Rico, Virgin Islands, Canal Zone)
Rm. 1025, 341 Ninth Ave., New York, N.Y. 10001
(212) 971–5401

Region 3 (Delaware, District of Columbia, Maryland, Pennsylvania, Virginia, West Virginia)

Rm. 406, Penn Square Bldg., 1317 Filbert St., Philadelphia, Pa. 19107
(215) 597–7816

Region 4 (Alabama, Florida, Georgia, Kentucky, Mississippi, North Carolina, South Carolina, Tennessee)
1371 Peachtree St. N.E., Atlanta, Ga. 30309
(404) 526–5416

Region 5 (Illinois, Indiana, Michigan, Minnesota, Ohio, Wisconsin)
300 South Wacker Dr., Chicago, Ill. 60606
(312) 353–7226

Region 6 (Arkansas, Louisiana, New Mexico, Oklahoma, Texas)

Rm. 687, 1100 Commerce St., Dallas, Tex. 75202
(214) 749–3641

Regions 7 and 8 (Colorado, Iowa, Kansas, Missouri, Montana, Nebraska, North Dakota, South Dakota, Utah, Wyoming)
Federal Office Bldg., 911 Walnut St., Kansas City, Mo. 64106)
(816) 374–2378

Regions 9 and 10 (Alaska, Arizona, California, Hawaii, Idaho, Nevada, Oregon, Washington)
450 Golden Gate Ave., P.O. Box 36107, San Francisco, California 94102)
(415) 556–3178

Labor-Management Services Administration
REGIONAL AND AREA OFFICES

California
Rm. 9061, Federal Office Bldg., 450 Golden Gate Ave., San Francisco, Calif. 94102
(415) 556–5915

Rm. 7731, Federal Bldg., 300 North Los Angeles St., Los Angeles, Calif. 90012
(213) 688–4975

Colorado
Suite 217, Brooks Tower, 1020–15th St., Denver, Colo. 80202
(303) 837–3203

District of Columbia
Rm. 509, Vanguard Bldg., 1111 20th St. N.W., Washington, D.C. 20210
(202) 961–4417

Florida
P.O. Box 3759, Norland Br., 18350 N.W. 2nd Ave., Miami, Fla. 33130
(305) 350–4611

Georgia
Rm. 300, 1371 Peachtree St. N.E., Atlanta, Ga. 30309
(404) 526–5237

APPENDIX

Hawaii
Rm. 601, 1833 Kalakaua Ave., Honolulu, Hawaii 96815
(808) 955-0259

Illinois
Rm. 848, Federal Office Bldg., 219 South Dearborn St., Chicago, Ill. 60604
(312) 353-1920

Louisiana
Rm. 940, Federal Office Bldg., 600 South St., New Orleans, La. 70130
(504) 527-6174

Massachusetts
Rm. 211, New Studio Bldg., 110 Tremont St., Boston, Mass. 02108
(617) 223-6736

Michigan
Rm. 1906, Washington Blvd., 234 State St., Detroit, Mich. 48226
(313) 226-6200

Minnesota
Rm. 110, Federal Courts Bldg., 110 South Fourth St., Minneapolis, Minn. 55401
(612) 745-2591

Missouri
Rm. 2511, Federal Office Bldg., 911 Walnut St., Kansas City, Mo. 64106
(816) 374-5131

Rm. 570, 210 North 12th Blvd., St. Louis, Mo. 63101
(314) 622-4691

New Jersey
Rm. 305, 9 Clinton St., Newark, N.J. 07102
(201) 645-3712

New York
Rm. 616, Federal Bldg., 111 West Huron St., Buffalo, N.W. 14202
(716) 842-3260

Rm. 3515, 1515 Broadway, New York, N.Y. 10036
(212) 971-7031

Ohio
Rm. 821, Federal Office Bldg., 1240 East Ninth St., Cleveland, Ohio 44199
(216) 522-3855

Pennsylvania
Rm. 1012, Penn Square Bldg., 1317 Filbert St., Philadelphia, Pa. 19107
(215) 597-7780

Rm. 2002, Federal Office Bldg., 1000 Liberty Ave., Pittsburgh, Pa. 15222
(412) 644-2925

Puerto Rico
Rm. 704, Condominia San Alberto, 605 Condado Ave., Santurce, P.R. 00907
(809) 723-8790

Tennessee
Rm. 825, 1808 West End Bldg., Nashville, Tenn. 37203
(615) 749-5906

Texas
Rm. 301, P.O. Bldg., Bryan and Ervay Sts., P.O. Box 239, Dallas, Tex. 75221
(214) 749-2886

Washington
Rm 3301, Smith Tower Bldg., 506 Second Ave., Seattle, Wash. 98104
(206) 442-5216

Manpower Administration
REGIONAL OFFICES

California (Arizona, California, Guam, Hawaii, and Nevada)
Federal Bldg., Rm. 10108, 450 Golden Gate Ave., San Francisco, Calif. 94102
(415) 556-7414

Colorado (Colorado, Montana, North Dakota, South Dakota, Utah, Wyoming)
16015 Federal Office Bldg., 1961 Stout St., Denver, Colo. 80202
(303) 837-4477

District of Columbia
Manpower Training and Employment Services Administration for D.C. District Bldg., Rm. 220, 14th and E Sts. N.W., Washington, D.C. 20004 (202) 629-3663

Georgia (Alabama, Florida, Georgia, Kentucky, Mississippi, North Carolina, South Carolina, Tennessee)
1371 Peachtree St. N.E., Rm. 700, Atlanta, Ga. 30309
(404) 526-5411

Illinois (Illinois, Indiana, Minnesota, Michigan, Ohio, Wisconsin)
300 South Wacker Dr., Chicago, Ill. 60606
(312) 353-4132

Massachusetts (Connecticut, Maine, Massachusetts, New Hampshire, Rhode Island, Vermont)
Rm. 1703, John F. Kennedy Bldg., Government Center, Boston, Mass. 02203
(617) 223-6439.

Missouri (Iowa, Kansas, Missouri, Nebraska, Colorado, Montana, North Dakota, South Dakota, Utah, Wyoming)
Federal Bldg., Rm. 3000, 911 Walnut St., Kansas City, Mo. 64106
(816) 374-3796

New York (New York, New Jersey, Puerto Rico, Virgin Islands)
341 Ninth Ave., Rm. 716, New York, N.Y. 10001
(212) 971-5445

Pennsylvania (Delaware, Maryland, Pennsylvania, Virginia, West Virginia)
P.O. Box 8796, Philadelphia, Pa. 19101
(215) 438-5200

Texas (Arkansas, Louisiana, New Mexico, Oklahoma, Texas)
Federal Bldg., U.S. Court House, 1100 Commerce St., Dallas, Tex. 75202
(214) 749-2841

Washington (Alaska, Idaho, Oregon, Washington)
2154 Arcade Plaza, 1321 Second Ave.. Seattle, Wash. 98101
(206) 442-7700

State Employment Security Agencies

Alabama
Industrial Relations Bldg., Montgomery, Ala. 36104
(205) 269-6417

Alaska
Department of Labor, P.O. Box 3-7000, Juneau, Alaska 99801
(907) 586-6500

Arizona
1717 West Jefferson St., P.O. Box 6339, Phoenix, Ariz. 85007
(602) 271-4900

Arkansas
Department of Labor, Employment Security Welfare Bldg., Box 2981, Little Rock, Ark. 72203
(501) 371-2121

California
800 Capitol Mall, Sacramento, Calif. 95814
(916) 445-8008

Colorado
1210 Sherman St., Denver, Colo. 80203
(303) 222-1551

Connecticut
Hartford, Conn. 06115
(203) 566-4280

Delaware
801 West St., Wilmington, Del. 19899
(302) 658-4331

District of Columbia
Employment Security Bldg., Sixth & Pennsylvania Ave. N.W., Washington, D.C. 20001
(202) 393-7915

APPENDIX

Florida
Florida Department of Commerce, Caldwell Bldg., Tallahassee, Fla. 32304
(904) 599–8211

Georgia
State Labor Bldg., Atlanta, Ga. 30334
(404) 656–3011

Guam
Department of Labor, Agana, Guam 96910

Hawaii
Dept. of Labor and Industrial Relations, 825 Mililani St., Honolulu, Hawaii 96813
(808) 531–3771

Idaho
317 Main St., P.O. Box 7189, Boise, Idaho 83707
(208) 344–7451

Illinois
Department of Labor, 165 North Canal St., Rm. 200, Chicago, Ill. 60606
(312) 793–4000

Indiana
10 North Senate Ave., Indianapolis, Ind. 46204
(317) 633–6961

Iowa
1000 East Grand Ave., Des Moines, Iowa 50319
(515) 281–5364

Kansas
State Labor Department, 401 Topeka Blvd., Topeka, Kans. 66603
(913) 232–4161

Kentucky
Dept. of Economic Security, New Capitol Annex Bldg., Frankfort, Ky. 40601
(502) 565–4258

Louisiana
Employment Security Bldg., 1001 North 23d St., P.O. Box 44094, Capital Station, Baton Rouge, La. 70804
(504) 348–2192

Maine
20 Union St., Augusta, Maine 04330
(207) 289–3814

Maryland
1100 North Eutaw St., Baltimore, Md. 21201
(301) 383–5600

Massachusetts
Charles F. Hurley Employment Security Bldg., Government Center, Boston, Mass. 02114
(617) 727–6600

Michigan
Department of Labor, 510 Blvd. Bldg., 7310 Woodward Ave., Detroit, Mich. 48202
(313) 872–4900

Minnesota
390 North Robert St., St. Paul, Minn. 55101
(612) 221–3711

Mississippi
1520 West Capitol St., P.O. Box 1699, Jackson, Miss. 39205
(601) 352–7631

Missouri
Department of Labor and Industrial Relations, 421 East Dunklin St., Jefferson City, Mo. 65101
(314) 636–6141

Montana
P.O. Box 1728, Helena, Mont. 59601
(406) 449–2511

Nebraska
Dept. of Labor, 550 South 16th St., P.O. Box 4600, State House Station, Lincoln, Nebr. 68509
(402) 432–6511

Nevada
500 East Third St., Carson City, Nev. 89701
(702) 882–7206

New Hampshire
32 South Main St., Concord, N.H. 03301
(603) 225–6671

New Jersey
John Fitch Plaza, P.O. Box V, Trenton, N.J.
08625
(609) 292–2121

New Mexico
The National Bldg., 505 Marquette N.W.
P.O. Box 1928, Albuquerque, N. Mex.
87103
(505) 842–8711

New York
Department of Labor, State Office Bldg.,
Campus, Albany, N.Y. 12201
(518) 457–2192

North Carolina
P.O. Box 25, 903 Jones and North McDowell
Sts., Raleigh, N.C. 27611
(919) 829–1110

North Dakota
201 East Broadway, P.O. Box 1537, Bismarck, N. Dak. 58501
(701) 244–2837

Ohio
145 South Front St., P.O. Box 1618, Columbus, Ohio 43216
(614) 469–2000

Oklahoma
Will Rogers Memorial Office Bldg., Oklahoma City, Okla. 73105
(405) 521–3794

Oregon
403 Labor and Industries Bldg., Salem,
Oreg. 97310
(503) 378–3209

Pennsylvania
Dept. of Labor and Industry Bldg., 7th and
Forster Sts., Harrisburg, Pa. 17121
(717) 787–6223

Puerto Rico
414 Barbosa Ave., Hato Rey, P.R. 00917
(809) 765–3030

Rhode Island
24 Mason St., Providence, R.I. 02903
(401) 861–6200

South Carolina
1225 Laurel St., P.O. Box 995, Columbia,
S.C. 29202
(803) 758–2583

South Dakota
607 North Fourth St., Aberdeen, S. Dak.
57401
(605) 622–2329

Tennessee
Cordell Hull State Office Bldg, Nashville,
Tenn. 37219
(615) 741–2131

Texas
TEC Bldg., Austin, Tex. 78701
(512) 472–6251

Utah
Industrial Commission, 174 Social Hall Ave.,
P.O. Box 11249, Salt Lake City, Utah 84111
(801) 322–1433

Vermont
Green Mountain Drive, PO. Box 488, Montpelier, Vt. 05602
(802) 229–0311

Virginia
703 East Main St., P.O. Box 1358, Richmond, Va. 23211
(703) 770–3001

Virgin Islands
P.O. Box 1092, Charlotte Amalie, St.
Thomas, V.I. 00801
(809) 774–1440

Washington
Employment Security Bldg, P.O. Box 367,
Olympia, Wash. 98501
(206) 753–5000

West Virginia
State Office Bldg., California and Washington Sts., Charleston, W.Va. 25305
(304) 348–2630

Wisconsin
4802 Sheboygan Ave., P.O. Box 1607, Madison, Wis. 53701
(608) 266–6131

Wyoming
ESC Bldg., Center and Midwest Sts., P.O.
Box 760, Casper, Wyo. 82601
(307) 237–3701

APPENDIX

CIVIL SERVICE COMMISSION
REGIONAL OFFICES

Region 1 (Boston Region: Connecticut, Maine, Massachusetts, New Hampshire, Rhode Island, Vermont)
Post Office and Courthouse Bldg., Boston, Mass. 02109
(617) 223-6240

Region 2 (New York Region: New Jersey, New York, Puerto Rico, Virgin Islands)
New Federal Bldg., 26 Federal Plaza, New York, N.Y. 10007
(212) 264-0440

Region 3 (Philadelphia Region: Delaware, District of Columbia, Maryland, Pennsylvania, Virginia, West Virginia)
Customhouse, Second and Chestnut Sts., Philadelphia, Pa. 19106
(215) 597-4543

Region 4 (Atlanta Region: Alabama, Florida, Georgia, Kentucky, Mississippi, North Carolina, South Carolina, Tennessee)
Atlanta Merchandise Mart, 240 Peachtree St. N.W., Atlanta, Ga. 30303
(404) 526-4261

Region 5 (Chicago Region: Illinois, Indiana, Michigan, Minnesota, Ohio, Wisconsin)
433 West Van Buren St., Chicago, Ill. 60607
(312) 353-2901

Region 6 (Dallas Region: Arkansas, Louisiana, New Mexico, Oklahoma, Texas)
1100 Commerce St., Dallas, Tex. 75202
(214) 749-352

Region 7 (St. Louis Region: Iowa, Kansas, Missouri, Nebraska)
1256 Federal Bldg., 1520 Market St., St. Louis, Mo. 63103
(314) 622-4262

Region 8 (Denver Region: Colorado, Montana, North Dakota, South Dakota, Utah, Wyoming)
Building 20, Denver Federal Center, Denver, Colo. 80225
(303) 234-2023

Region 9 (San Francisco Region: Arizona, California, Hawaii, Nevada, Pacific Area)
Federal Bldg., Box 3610, 450 Golden Gate Ave., San Francisco, Calif. 94102
(415) 556-0581

Region 10 (Seattle Region: Alaska, Idaho, Oregon, Washington)
3004 Federal Office Bldg., First Ave. and Madison St., Seattle, Wash. 98104
(206) 442-7537

AREA OFFICES AND JOB INFORMATION CENTERS

Region 1
Federal Bldg., Augusta, Maine 04330
(207) 622-6269

Post Office and Courthouse Bldg., Rm. 1004, Boston, Mass. 02109
(617) 223-2571

Federal Bldg., Elmwood Ave., and Pearl St., Burlington, Vt. 05401
(802) 862-6501, Ext. 259

Rm. 716, Federal Bldg., 450 Main St., Hartford, Conn. 06103
(203) 244-3096

Federal Bldg., U.S. Post Office, Daniel and Penhallow Sts., Portsmouth, N.H. 03801
(603) 436-7720, Ext. 762

Federal Bldg., and U.S. Post Office, Kennedy Plaza, Providence, R.I. 02903
(401) 528-4447

Region 2
Pan Am Bldg., 255 Ponce de Leon Ave., Hato Rey, P.R. 00917

Federal Office Bldg., Rm. 936, 970 Broad St., Newark, N.J. 07102
(201) 645-3673

Federal Bldg., 26 Federal Plaza, New York, N.Y. 10007
(212) 264-0422

O'Donnell Bldg., 301 Erie Blvd. West, Syracuse, N.Y. 13202
(315) 473-5660

Region 3
Federal Office Bldg., Lombard St. and Hopkins Pl., Baltimore, Md. 21261
(301) 962-3822

Federal Bldg., 500 Quarrier St., Charleston, W. Va. 25301
(304) 343-6181, Ext. 226

Atlantic National Bank Bldg., 415 St. Paul Blvd., Norfolk, Va. 23510
(703) 625-6515

Federal Bldg., 128 North Broad St., Philadelphia, Pa. 19102
(215) 597-7440

Federal Bldg., 1000 Liberty Ave., Pittsburgh, Pa. 15222
(412) 644-2755

U.S. Post Office and Courthouse, 11th and King Sts., Wilmington, Del. 19801
(302) 658-6911, Ext. 540

Region 4
275 Peachtree St., N.E., Atlanta, Ga. 30303
(404) 526-4315

Federal Office Bldg., 334 Meeting St., Charleston, S.C. 29403
(803) 577-4171, Ext. 328

Southerland Bldg., 806 Governors Dr., S.W., Huntsville, Ala. 35801
(205) 453-5070

802 North State St., Jackson, Miss. 39201
(601) 948-7821

Rm. 167, Federal Bldg., 600 Federal Pl., Louisville, Ky. 40202
(502) 582-5130

Federal Bldg., 451 College St., Macon, Ga. 31201
(912) 743-0381, Ext. 2401

Federal Office Bldg., 167 North Main St., Memphis, Tenn. 38103
(901) 534-3956

First National Bank Bldg., 107 St. Francis St., Rm. 1802, Mobile, Ala. 36602
(205) 433-3581

3101 Maguire Bldg., Orlando, Fla. 32803
(305) 425-0511

310 New Bern Ave., Federal Office Bldg., Raleigh, N.C. 27611
(919) 755-4361

Region 5
Rm. 1322, 219 Dearborn St. South, Chicago, Ill. 60604
(312) 353-5136

New Federal Bldg., 1240 East Ninth St., Cleveland, Ohio 44199
(216) 522-4232

40 West Fourth St., Rm. 600, Grant-Deneau Bldg., Dayton, Ohio 45402
(513) 461-4830, Ext. 5540

144 West Lafayette St., Rm. 1026, Detroit, Mich. 48226
(313) 226-6950

Rm. 102, 36 South Pennsylvania St., Indianapolis, Ind. 46204
(317) 633-8662

161 West Wisconsin Ave., Rm. 215, Milwaukee, Wis. 53203
(414) 272-8600, Ext. 3761

Rm. 196, Federal Bldg., Fort Snelling, Twin Cities, Minn. 55111
(612) 725-3355

Federal Office Bldg., Rm. 1523, 550 Main St., Cincinnati, Ohio 45202
(513) 684–2351

Bldg. No. 3400, Electronics Supply Office, Great Lakes, Ill. 60088
(312) 688–4620

Bldg. 103, Rock Island Arsenal, Rock Island, Ill. 61201
(309) 794–4322

Region 6
Federal Bldg., 421 Gold Ave., S.W., Albuquerque, N. Mex. 87101
(505) 843–2557

Rm. 103, 1100 Commerce St., Dallas, Tex. 75202
(214) 749–3156

El Paso National Bank Bldg., 411 North Stanton St., El Paso, Tex. 79901
(915) 533–9351, Ext. 5388

702 Caroline St., Houston, Tex. 77002
(713) 226–5501

Rm. 3305, Federal Office Bldg., 700 West Capitol Ave., Little Rock, Ark. 72201
(501) 372–5842

Federal Bldg. South, 600 South St., New Orleans, La. 70130
(504) 527–2764

210 Northwest Sixth St., Oklahoma City, Okla. 73102
(405) 231–4948

Federal Bldg., 615 East Houston St., San Antonio, Tex. 78205
(512) 225–5511, Ext. 343

Rm. 105, Downtown Postal Bldg., 701 North Upper Broadway, Corpus Christi, Tex. 78401
(512) 883–5363

819 Taylor St., Fort Worth, Tex. 76102
(817) 334–3484

Region 7
191 Federal Bldg., 210 Walnut St., Des Moines, Iowa 50309
(515) 284–4547

Rm. 129, Federal Bldg., 601 East 12th St., Kansas City, Mo. 64106
(816) 374–5702

Rm. 1014, U.S. Court and Post Office Bldg., 215 North 17th St., Omaha, Nebr. 68102
(402) 221–3815

Rm. 1712, Federal Bldg., 1520 Market St., St. Louis, Mo. 63103
(314) 622–4285

Rm. 101, One-Twenty Bldg., 120 South Market St., Wichita, Kans. 67202
(316) 267–6106

Region 8
Rm. 108, 1805 Capitol Ave., Cheyenne, Wyo. 82001
(307) 778–2220, Ext. 2108

Rm. 203, Post Office Bldg., 1823 Stout St., Denver, Colo. 80202
(303) 297–3506

Federal Bldg. and Post Office, Rm. 200, 657 Second Ave., Fargo, N. Dak. 58102
(701) 237–5197

IBM Bldg., 130 Neill Ave., Helena, Mont. 59601
(406) 442–388

Rm. 118, Dusek Bldg., 919 Main St., Rapid City, S. Dak. 57701
(605) 348–1261

Federal Bldg. Annex, 135 South State St., Salt Lake City, Utah 84111
(801) 524–5744

Region 9
Federal Bldg., Honolulu, Hawaii 96813
(808) 546–5967

Eastern Columbia Bldg., 851 South Broadway, Los Angeles, Calif. 90014
(213) 688–3360

Balke Bldg., 44 West Adams St., Phoenix, Ariz. 85003
(602) 261–4731

Rm. 1139, Federal Bldg., 300 Booth St., Reno, Nev. 89502
(702) 784-5535

650 Capitol Mall, Rm. 4210, Sacramento, Calif. 95814
(916) 449-3441

380 West Court St., San Bernardino, Calif. 92401
(714) 884-3111, Ext. 395

1400 Fifth Ave., Suite 304, San Diego, Calif. 92101
(714) 293-6165

450 Golden Gate Ave., Box 36122, San Francisco, Calif. 94102
(415) 556-6667

300 Las Vegas Blvd. South, Las Vegas, Nev. 89101
(702) 385-6345

1340 Pine Ave., Long Beach, Calif. 90813
(213) 591-2331

Rm. 207, Post Office Bldg., 120 West Cypress St., Santa Maria, Calif. 93454
(805) 925-9719

Region 10
Hill Bldg., 632 Sixth Ave., Anchorage, Alaska 99501
(907) 272-5561

Rm. 663, Federal Bldg., U.S. Courthouse, 550 West Fort St., Boise, Idaho 83702

319 Southwest Pine St., Portland, Oreg. 97204
(503) 221-3141

Federal Office Bldg., First Ave., Madison St., Seattle, Wash. 98104
(206) 583-4365

511 Burwell St., Bremerton, Wash. 98314
(206) 377-2995

Suite 7, Rampart Bldg., 529 Fifth Ave., Fairbanks, Alaska 99701
(907) 452-1603

ENVIRONMENTAL PROTECTION AGENCY
REGIONAL ADMINISTRATORS

Region 1 (Connecticut, Maine, Massachusetts, New Hampshire, Rhode Island, Vermont)
Rm. 2303, John F. Kennedy Federal Bldg., Government Center, Boston, Mass. 02203
(617) 223-7210

Region 2 (New Jersey, New York, Puerto Rico, Virgin Islands)
Rm. 847, 26 Federal Plaza, New York N.Y. 10007
(212) 264-2525

Region 3 (Delaware, District of Columbia, Maryland, Pennsylvania, Virginia, West Virginia)
Curtis Bldg., 6th and Walnut Sts., Philadelphia, Pa. 19106
(215) 597-9800

Region 4 (Alabama, Florida, Georgia, Kentucky, Mississippi, North Carolina, South Carolina, Tennessee)
Suite 300, 1421 Peachtree St. N.E., Atlanta, Ga. 30309
(404) 526-5727

Region 5 (Illinois, Indiana, Michigan, Minnesota, Ohio, Wisconsin)
On North Wacker Dr., Rm. 900, Chicago, Ill. 60605
(312) 353-5250

Region 6 (Arkansas, Louisiana, New Mexico, Oklahoma, Texas)
1600 Patterson St., Dallas, Tex. 85202
(214) 749-1962

APPENDIX

Region 7 (Iowa, Kansas, Missouri, Nebraska)
1735 Baltimore Ave., Rm. 249, Kansas City, Mo. 64108
(816) 374-5493

Region 8 (Colorado, Montana, North Dakota, South Dakota, Utah, Wyoming)
Rm. 953, Lincoln Tower Bldg., 1860 Lincoln St., Denver, Colo. 80203
(303) 837-3847

Region 9 (Arizona, California, Hawaii, Nevada, American Samoa, Guam, Trust Territories of Pacific Islands, Wake Island)
100 California St., San Francisco, Calif. 94111
(415) 556-2320

Region 10 (Alaska, Idaho, Oregon, Washington)
1200 6th Ave., Seattle, Wash. 98101
(206) 442-1200

EQUAL EMPLOYMENT OPPORTUNITY COMMISSION
REGIONAL OFFICES

California
San Francisco Regional Office, 2d Floor, Bldg., 6, 620 Central Ave., Alameda, Calif. 94501
(415) 273-7177

Georgia
Atlanta Regional Office, Citizens' Trust Bldg., 11th Floor, 75 Piedmont Ave., N.W. Atlanta, Ga. 30303
(404) 526-6991

Illinois
Chicago Regional Office, 600 South Michigan Ave., Rm. 611, Chicago, Ill. 60605
(312) 353-1488

Missouri
Kansas City Regional Office, Rm. 513, 911 Walnut St., Kansas City, Mo. 64106
(816) 374-3781

New York
New York Regional Office, Federal Office Bldg., Rm. 4000, 26 Federal Plaza, New York, N.Y. 10007
(212) 264-3640

Pennsylvania
Philadelphia Regional Office, Jefferson Bldg., 1015 Chestnut St., Philadelphia, Pa. 19107
(215) 597-2327

Texas
Dallas Regional Office, Rm. 5A4, 1100 Commerce St., Dallas, Tex. 75202
(214) 749-1841

GENERAL SERVICES ADMINISTRATION
REGIONAL OFFICES

Region 1 (Connecticut, Maine, Massachusetts, New Hampshire, Rhode Island, Vermont)
620 Post Office and Courthouse Bldg., Boston, Mass. 02109
(617) 223-2601

Region 2 (New Jersey, New York, Puerto Rico, Virgin Islands)
26 Federal Plaza, New York, N.Y. 10007
(212) 264-2600

Region 3 (Delaware, District of Columbia, Maryland, Pennsylvania, Virginia, West Virginia)
Seventh and D Sts., S.W. Washington, D.C. 20407
(202) 963-6146

Region 4 (Alabama, Florida, Georgia, Kentucky, Mississippi, North Carolina, South Carolina, Tennessee)

1776 Peachtree St. N.W., Atlanta, Ga. 30309
(404) 526-5600

Region 5 (Illinois, Indiana, Michigan, Minnesota, Ohio, Wisconsin)
219 South Dearborn St., Chicago, Ill. 60604
(312) 353-5395

Region 6 (Arkansas, Louisiana, New Mexico, Oklahoma, Texas)
19 Taylor St., Fort Worth, Tex. 76102
(817) 334-2321

Region 7 (Iowa, Kansas, Missouri, Nebraska)
1500 East Bannister Rd., Kansas City, Mo. 64131
(816) 361-7201

Region 8 (Colorado, Montana, North Dakota, South Dakota, Utah, Wyoming)
Bldg., 41, Denver Federal Center, Denver, Colo. 80225
(303) 234-4171

Region 9 (Arizona, California, Hawaii, Nevada)
49 Fourth St., San Francisco, Calif. 94103
(415) 556-3221

Region 10 (Alaska, Idaho, Oregon, Washington)
Regional Headquarters Bldg., GSA Center, Auburn, Wash. 98002
(206) 833-5223

FEDERAL INFORMATION CENTERS

Arizona
Federal Bldg., 230 N. First Ave., Phoenix, Ariz. 85025
(602) 261-3313

California
Federal Bldg., 300 North Los Angeles St., Los Angeles, Calif. 90012
(213) 688-3800

202 C. St., San Diego, Calif. 92101
(714) 293-6030

Federal Bldg., U.S. Courthouse, 450 Golden Gate Ave., San Francisco, Calif. 94102
(415) 556-6600

Colorado
Federal Bldg., U.S. Courthouse, 1961 Stout St., Denver, Colo. 80202
(303) 837-3602

Florida
Federal Bldg., 51 Southwest First Ave., Miami, Fla. 33130
(305) 350-4155

William C. Cramer Federal Bldg., 144 First Ave., St. Petersburg, Fla. 33701
(813) 893-3495

Georgia
Federal Bldg., 275 Peachtree St., N.E., Atlanta, Ga. 30303
(404) 526-6891

Hawaii
U.S. Post Office, Courthouse and Customhouse, 335 Merchant St., Honolulu, Hawaii 96813
(808) 546-8620

Illinois
Everett McKinley Dirksen Bldg., 219 South Dearborn St., Chicago, Ill. 60604
(312) 353-4242

Indiana
Federal Bldg., U.S. Courthouse, 46 East Ohio St., Indianapolis, Ind. 46204
(317) 633-8484

Kentucky
Federal Bldg., 600 Federal Pl., Louisville, Ky. 40202
(502) 582-6261

Louisiana
Federal Bldg., U.S. Post Office, 701 Loyola Ave., New Orleans, La. 70113
(504) 527-6696

Maryland
Federal Bldg., 31 Hopkins Plaza, Baltimore, Md. 21201
(301) 962–4980

Massachusetts
John F. Kennedy Federal Bldg., Boston, Mass. 02203
(617) 223–7121

Michigan
Federal Bldg., U.S. Courthouse, 231 West Lafayette St., Detroit, Mich. 48226
(313) 226–7016

Minnesota
Federal Bldg., U.S. Courthouse, 110 South Fourth St., Minneapolis, Minn. 55401
(612) 725–2073

Missouri
Federal Bldg., 601 East 12th St., Kansas City, Mo. 64106
(816) 374–2466

Federal Bldg., 1520 Market St., St. Louis, Mo. 63103
(314) 662–4106

Nebraska
Rm. 1205, Federal Bldg., U.S. Post Office and Court House, 215 North 17th St., Omaha, Nebr. 68102
(402) 221–3353

New Jersey
Federal Bldg., 970 Broad St., Newark, N.J. 07102
(201) 645–3600

New Mexico
Federal Bldg., U.S. Courthouse, 500 Gold Ave., S.W., Albuquerque, N. Mex. 87101
(505) 843–3091

New York
U.S. Courthouse, 111 West Huron St., Buffalo, N.Y. 14202
(716) 842–5770

Federal Office Bldg., U.S. Customs Court, 26 Federal Plaza, New York, N.Y. 10007
(212) 264–4464

Ohio
Federal Bldg., 550 Main St., Cincinnati, Ohio 45202
(513) 684–2801

Federal Bldg., 1240 East Ninth St., Cleveland, Ohio 44199
(216) 522–4040

Oklahoma
Rm. 115, U.S. Post Office and Federal Office Bldg., 201 Northwest Third St., Oklahoma City, Okla. 73102
(405) 231–4868

Oregon
U.S. Courthouse, 620 Southwest Main St., Portland, Oreg. 97205
(503) 221–2222

Pennsylvania
One East Penn Square Bldg., 17 North Juniper St., Philadelphia, Pa. 19107
(215) 597–7042

Federal Bldg., 1000 Liberty Ave., Pittsburgh, Pa. 15222
(412) 644–3456

Tennessee
Clifford Davis Federal Bldg., 167 N. Main St., Memphis, Tenn. 38103
(901) 534–3285

Texas
Fritz Garland Lanham Federal Bldg., 819 Taylor, St., Fort Worth, Tex. 76102
(817) 334–3624

Federal Bldg., U.S. Courthouse, 515 Rusk Ave., Houston, Tex. 77002
(713) 226–5711

Utah
Federal Bldg., U.S. Post Office, Courthouse, 125 South State St., Salt Lake City, Utah 84111
(801) 524–5353

Washington
Arcade Plaza, 1321 Second Ave., Seattle, Wash. 98101
(206) 442–0570

How to Get What You Want from the U.S. Government

NATIONAL ARCHIVES AND RECORDS SERVICE

NATIONAL ARCHIVES

Central Reference Division
The National Archives, Washington, D.C. 20408
(202) 963–6413

PRESIDENTIAL LIBRARIES

Iowa
Herbert Hoover Library, West Branch, Iowa 52358
(319) 643–5301

Kansas
Dwight D. Eisenhower Library, Abilene, Kans. 67410
(913) 827–9738

Massachusetts
John F. Kennedy Library, 380 Trapelo Rd., Waltham, Mass. 02154
(617) 223–7250

Missouri
Harry S. Truman Library, Independence, Mo. 64050
(816) 374–6235

New York
Franklin D. Roosevelt Library, Hyde Park, N.Y. 12538
(914) 229–8114

Texas
Lyndon B. Johnson Library, Austin, Tex. 78712
(512) 397–5137

SMALL BUSINESS ADMINISTRATION
REGIONAL OFFICES

Region 1 (Connecticut, Maine, Massachusetts, New Hampshire, Rhode Island, Vermont)
John F. Kennedy Federal Bldg., Rm. 2113
Boston. Mass. 02203
(617) 223–6660

Region 2 (New Jersey, New York, Puerto Rico, Virgin Islands)
26 Federal Plaza, Rm. 3930, New York, N.Y. 10007
(212) 264–1450

Region 3 (Delaware, District of Columbia, Maryland, Pennsylvania, Virginia, West Virginia)
1 Decker Square, East Lobby, Suite 400, Bala Cynwyd, Pa. 19004
(215) 597–3201

Region 4 (Alabama, Florida, Georgia, Kentucky, Mississippi, North Carolina, South Carolina, Tennessee)
1401 Peachtree St., N.E., Rm. 441, Atlanta, Ga. 30309
(404) 526–5679

Region 5 (Illinois, Indiana, Michigan, Minnesota, Ohio, Wisconsin)
Federal Bldg., 219 South Dearborn St., Rm. 437, Chicago, Ill. 60604
(312) 353–4490

Region 6 (Arkansas, Louisiana, New Mexico, Oklahoma, Texas)
1100 Commerce St., Rm. 300, Dallas, Tex. 75202
(214) 749–1263

APPENDIX

Region 7 (Iowa, Kansas, Missouri, Nebraska)
911 Walnut St., 24th Floor, Kansas City, Mo. 64106
(816) 374–3316

Region 8 (Colorado, Montana, North Dakota, South Dakota, Utah, Wyoming)
721 19th St., Rm. 426A, Denver, Colo. 80202
(303) 837–4021

Region 9 (Arizona, California, Hawaii, Nevada, Pacific Islands)
Federal Bldg., 450 Golden Gate Ave., San Francisco, Calif. 94102
(415) 556–7487

Region 10 (Alaska, Idaho, Oregon, Washington)
710 2nd Ave., 5th Floor, Dexter Horton Bldg., Seattle, Wash. 98104
(206) 442–5676

VETERANS ADMINISTRATION
Veterans' Benefits
FIELD OFFICES

Alabama
Regional Office, Aronov Bldg., 474 South Court St., Montgomery, Ala. 36104
(205) 263–7201, 7202

Alaska
VA Office, Loussac-Sogn Bldg., 429 D St., Anchorage, Alaska 99501
(907) 279–3561

Regional Office, Federal Bldg., U.S. Post Office and Courthouse, 709 West Ninth St., Juneau, Alaska 99801
(907) 586–7472

Arizona
Regional Office, Federal Bldg., 230 North First Ave., Phoenix, Ariz. 85025
(602) 261–4771

Arkansas
Regional Office, Federal Office Bldg., 700 West Capitol Ave., Little Rock, Ark. 72201
(501) 378–5231, 5232

California
Veterans Assistance Center, 101 South Willowbrook Ave., Compton, Calif. 90220
(213) 537–3202

Regional Office, Federal Bldg., 11000 Wilshire Blvd., Los Angeles, Calif. 90024
(213) 824–7237

VA Office, Wausaw Medical Bldg., 2131 Third Ave., San Diego, Calif. 92101
(714) 293–6238

Regional Office, 49 Fouth St., San Francisco, Calif. 94103
(415) 556–9000

Colorado
Regional Office, Denver Federal Center, Denver, Colo. 80225
(303) 234–4089

Connecticut
Regional Office, 450 Main St., Hartford, Conn. 06103
(203) 244–3740

Delaware
VA Center, 1601 Kirkwood Hwy., Wilmington, Del. 19805
(302) 658–7291

District of Columbia
Veterans Benefits Office, 2033 M. St., N.W., Washington, D.C. 20421
(202) 347–1121

Veterans Assistance Center, 25 K St., N.E., Washington, D.C. 20002
(202) 638–2966

Florida
VA Office, Post Office and Courthouse Bldg., 311 West Monroe St., Jacksonville, Fla. 32201
(904) 791–2756–57

VA Office, 51 Southwest First Ave., Miami, Fla. 33130
(305) 351-5167-68

Regional Office, Federal Bldg., 144 First Ave., South, St. Petersburg, Fla. 33701
(813) 893-3131

Georgia
Regional Office, 730 Peachtree St., N.E., Atlanta, Ga. 30308
(404) 526-3615

Hawaii
Regional Office, 680 Ala Moana Blvd., Honolulu, Hawaii 96801
(808) 546-5991

Idaho
Regional Office, Federal Bldg. and U.S. Courthouse, 550 West Fort St. Box 044, Boise, Idaho 83702
(205) 324-6581

Illinois
Regional Office, 2030 West Taylor St., Chicago, Ill. 60680
(312) 353-4400

Indiana
Regional Office, 36 South Pa. St., Indianapolis, Ind. 46204
(317) 633-7000

Iowa
Regional Office, Federal Office Bldg., 210 Walnut St., Des Moines, Iowa 50309
(515) 284-4000

Kansas
VA Center, 5500 East Kellogg, Wichita, Kans. 67218
(316) 685-2221

Kentucky
Regional Office, 600 Federal Place, Louisville, Ky. 40202
(502) 582-5803, 5801

Louisiana
Regional Office, 701 Loyola Ave., New Orleans, La. 70113
(504) 527-6492

VA Office, 510 East Stoner Ave., Shreveport, La. 71101
(318) 527-2985

Maine
VA Office, 76 Pearl St., Portland, Maine 04111
(207) 775-3223

VA Center, Togus, Maine 04330
(207) 623-8411

Maryland
Regional Office, Federal Bldg., 31 Hopkins Plaza, Baltimore, Md. 21201
(301) 962-4686

Massachusetts
Regional Office, John F. Kennedy Federal Bldg., Government Center, Boston, Mass. 02203
(617) 223-3080

VA Office, 1200 Main St., Springfield, Mass. 01103
(413) 781-2420

Michigan
Regional Office, 801 West Baltimore and Third Sts., Detroit, Mich. 48232
(313) 874-2340

Minnesota
VA Center, Federal Bldg., Fort Snelling, St. Paul, Minn. 55111
(612) 725-4242

Mississippi
VA Center, 1500 East Woodrow Wilson Dr., Jackson, Miss. 39216
(601) 362-1201, 1203

Missouri
VA Office, Federal Office Bldg., 601 East 12th St., Kansas City, Mo. 64106
(816) 374-5761

Regional Office, Federal Bldg., 1520 Market St., St. Louis, Mo. 63103
(314) 622-8100

Montana
VA Center, Fort Harrison, Mont. 59636
(406) 442–6410

Nebraska
Regional Office, 220 South 17th St., Lincoln,
Nebr. 68508
(402) 475–2611

Nevada
VA Center, 1000 Locust St., Reno, Nev.
89502
(702) 784–5587

New Hampshire
Regional Office, 497 Silver St., Manchester,
N.H. 03103
(603) 669–7011

New Jersey
Regional Office, 20 Washington Place, Newark, N.J. 07102
(201) 645–3000

New Mexico
Regional Office, 500 Gold Ave., S.W., Albuquerque, N. Mex. 87101
(505) 843–0311

New York
VA Office, Executive Park, North Stuyvesant Plaza, Albany, N.Y. 12201
(518) 472–4206

Regional Office, 111 West Huron St., Buffalo, N.Y. 14202
(716) 842–2285

Regional Office, 252 Seventh Ave., New
York York City 10001
(212) 620–6901

VA Office, 39 State St., Rochester, N.Y.
14614
(716) 546–1303

VA Office, 809 South Salina St., Syracuse,
N.Y. 13202
(315) 473–2680

North Carolina
Regional Office, Wachovia Bldg., 301 North
Main St., Winston-Salem, N.C. 27102
(919) 723–2201

North Dakota
VA Center, 21st Ave., and Elm St., Fargo,
N. Dak. 58102
(701) 232–3241

Ohio
VA Office, Federal Office Bldg., 550 Main
St., Cincinnati, Ohio 45202
(513) 684–2624

Regional Office, Federal Office Bldg., 1240
East Ninth St., Cleveland, Ohio 44199
(216) 522–3131

VA Office, Bryson Bldg., 700 Bryden Rd.,
Columbus, Ohio 43215
(614) 469–7336

Oklahoma
Regional Office, Second and Court Sts.,
Muskogee, Okla. 74401
(918) 683–3111

VA Office, Federal Bldg., 200 Northwest
Fourth St., Oklahoma City, Okla. 73102
(405) 231–4115

Oregon
Regional Office, 426 Southwest Stark St.,
Portland, Oreg. 97204
(503) 226–3361

Pennsylvania
VA Center, 5000 Wissahickon Ave., Philadelphia, Pa. 19101
(215) 438–5225

Regional Office, 1000 Liberty Ave., Pittsburgh, Pa. 15222
(412) 644–6700

VA Office, 19–27 North Main St., Wilkes-Barre, Pa. 18701
(717) 825–6811

Philippines
Regional Office, 1131 Roxas Blvd., Manila,
Philippines 33781

Puerto Rico
VA Center, Barrio Monacillos, San Juan,
P.R. 00921
(809) 764–4545, 6980

Rhode Island
Regional Office, Federal Bldg., Kennedy Plaza, Providence, R.I. 02903
(401) 528-4431

South Carolina
Regional Office, 1801 Assembly St., Columbus, S.C. 29201
(803) 765-5607

South Dakota
VA Center, 2501 West 22nd St., Sioux Falls, S. Dak. 57101
(605) 336-3690

Tennessee
Regional Office, U.S. Courthouse, 801 Broadway, Nashville, Tenn. 37203
(615) 749-5261

Texas
VA Office, U.S. Courthouse and Federal Office Bldg., 1100 Commerce St., Dallas, Tex. 75202
(214) 748-5611

Regional Office, 515 Rusk Ave., Houston, Tex. 77061
(713) 226-4176

VA Office, Federal Bldg., 1205 Texas Ave., Lubbock, Tex. 79401
(765) 854-1258

VA Office, 410 South Main St., San Antonio, Tex. 78204
(512) 225-5511, Ext. 4841

Regional Office, 1400 North Valley Mills Dr., Waco, Tex. 76710
(817) 756-8732, 8733

Utah
Regional Office, 125 South State St., Salt Lake City, Utah 84111
(801) 524-5500

Vermont
VA Center, White River Jct., Vt. 05001
(802) 295-3131

Virginia
Regional Office, 211 West Campbell Ave., Roanoke, Va. 24011
(703) 343-6200, 6201

Washington
Regional Office, Sixth and Lenora Bldg., Seattle, Wash. 98121
(206) 682-9100

West Virginia
Regional Office, 502 Eighth St., Huntington, W. Va. 25701
(304) 529-2311

Wisconsin
Regional Office, 342 North Water St., Milwaukee, Wis. 53202
(414) 224-1101

Wyoming
VA Center, 2360 East Pershing Blvd., Cheyenne, Wyo. 82001
(307) 778-7550

INDEX

225

INDEX

INDEX